INTRODUCTION TO
BOBBIN LACE PATTERNS

C000156611

By the same author and published by Batsford:

Practical Skills in Bobbin Lace
The Torchon Lace Workbook

and, together with Geraldine Stott:

The Book of Bobbin Lace Stitches
100 Traditional Bobbin Lace Patterns
Introduction to Bobbin Lace Stitches

INTRODUCTION TO BOBBIN LACE PATTERNS

Bridget M Cook

B T Batsford Ltd, London

First published 1984
© Bridget M Cook 1984
First published in paperback 1991
Reprinted 1993

A catalogue record for this book is available from
the British Library.

ISBN 0 7134 4514 9

Typeset by Tek-Art Ltd, Kent
and printed in Hong Kong
for the Publishers,
B T Batsford Ltd
4 Fitzhardinge Street
London, W1H 0AH

EXPLANATORY NOTES

The tulle net is usually started and worked on the diagonal in Point Ground, but throughout the book most prickings are given straight starts to provide as long a pattern as possible.

Whole stitch

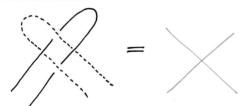

linen or whole stitch = cross
                      twist both pairs
                      cross

Half stitch

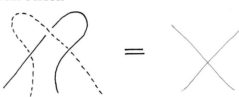

half stitch = cross
                twist both pairs

The net ground or tulle net

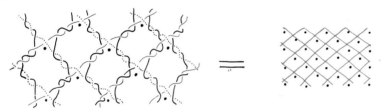

Always work cross, pin and twist both pairs ×3 at each pinhole.
Note that one thread from each pair travels diagonally right across the work in both directions, if worked accurately, with just 3 twists after each crossing.

Footside and catchpin stitch

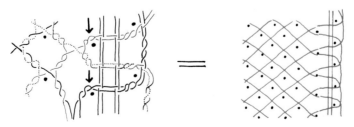

Footside and catchpin (catchpin marked with ↓). At the footside edge the worker pair is interchanged with the edge pair throughout the work every time the footside edge is reached. For the catchpin stitch the worker pair, after whole stitching through the 2 passive pairs, is twisted ×3, and pinned up before it is joined to the net with a net stitch. This makes the net go around the pin instead of being supported by the pin as in the rest of the net. This is an important feature of Point Ground work.

Catchpin – alternative use

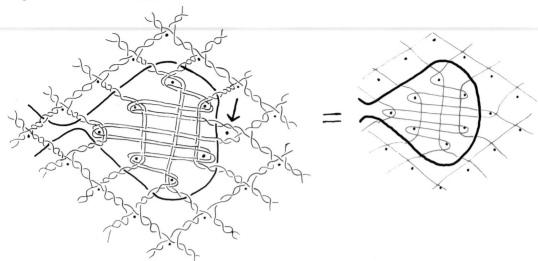

Catchpin stitch can also be used in order to make a neat joint between a whole stitch block and the net.

Single honeycomb stitch

twist ×2 both pairs
cross and pin
twist ×2 both pairs
cross
twist ×2 both pairs

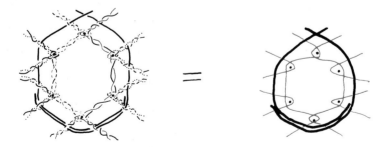

Honeycomb ring

This is worked in the honeycomb stitch from the top pin, then out to the right and left pins. One pair from each side then exchanges with a net pair on either side. The new pair from the net then works with the hanging pair on either side from the top, followed by the bottom pin to finish.

INTRODUCTION

This selection of practical lace patterns has been carefully chosen to illustrate varying techniques within the individual patterns. It will enable the lacemaker to have a greater choice in the range of stitches that are available in traditional Point Ground lace.

Point Ground is normally thought to be the most intricate and difficult of English laces but if the patterns are carefully analysed, as in the research for this book, then translated into diagrammatic form, the most intricate design is capable of being followed.

Originally researched from various museums and private collections in Great Britain, the patterns have been adapted and re-designed so as to create corners in addition to the original straight prickings. Some of the patterns have also been extended to enable collars, cuffs, circles and ovals to be made. Several of the patterns are individual motifs ideal for paperweights or wine-glass mats and the like.

The patterns are not arranged in degree of difficulty but, where possible, progress with the increasing number of bobbins used. The inexperienced would therefore be wise to begin with the earlier patterns requiring fewer bobbins and thus being less complex.

Arranged on either a single page or adjacent pages, each pattern is set out clearly with the pricking, a colour coded diagram and a photograph of the completed work. The colour coding enables the lacemaker to follow the design simply step-by-step.

These patterns have no particular original names and have been given names for identification purposes only.

Whilst few lacemakers will possess the necessary equipment or experience to construct a traditional pricking and to draw the difficult gimp lines from the original lace, in this book the Author has worked through these stages and has provided a clear pricking of each pattern.

It may be convenient for the prickings to be traced from the patterns in the book and pricked in the traditional manner but there is now an easier method which some may prefer to use: photocopiers are now freely available in many places and it is recommended that the prickings selected are photocopied. (This is acceptable only on the strict understanding that the photocopy taken is for the personal use of the lacemaker).

The thread used in making the illustrated laces in this book ranged from 180 cotton to 120 linen but the majority were made in DMC 50 cotton. It is impossible to recommend individual threads for the respective patterns as availability differs from time to time, and the lacemaker will therefore need to select the best available.

It will be seen that the illustrated prickings are shown to have a straight edge at the top but this is merely to provide the maximum length of pricking. It is normally best to start with a diagonal line.

ACKNOWLEDGEMENTS

The Author wishes to express her grateful thanks to her long-suffering husband and her kind friends and fellow lacemakers for their assistance in compiling the materials for this book. Too many to mention by name but, none the less, sincerely to be thanked for their kindness and helpfulness. Several will recognize their names attached to patterns within this book.

Bunched heading pairs

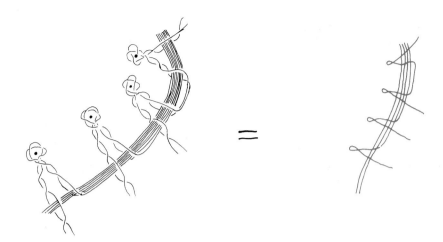

In a few patterns there are deep valleys and several pairs in the heading.
In these patterns, instead of working the pairs in the usual manner by whole stitching each pair in turn before working the picot, the pairs can be bunched together and passed between the workers in a gimp manner.
Pairs are taken in or out of the bunch when needed. This forms a neat, narrow, rolled edge which is quite firm.

False picot

A false picot is sometimes needed to start a motif or collar

lay 2 pairs horizontally across the work

twist ×5

place a pin under the twists and bring the pairs down to the working position

whole stitch the two pairs through each other

this completes the picot

this can also be made with 4 pairs if 4 pairs are needed

Collar/motif start

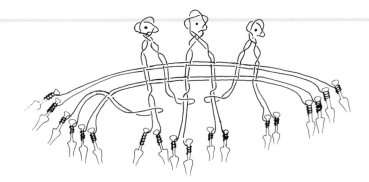

This is a method for starting a collar/motif where picots are required.
Make a false picot, lay 4 pairs horizontally across the work, work the false picot pairs down through them. These 4 pairs become the 2 pairs working either way and form the outside passive pairs which will go along the outer edge by the picots. In order to add a new pair slip the new pair up one of the false picot pairs and whole stitch through the 2 passive pairs. Make a picot and whole stitch back through these 2 pairs, slip the next new pair on to this pair and work up through the 2 passives – make a picot and work back. As many new pairs can be added in this way as needed.

Entry and exit of threads

▼   this indicates where a new thread or gimp is to be started

▲   this indicates where a thread or gimp is tied off.

Large honeycomb ring

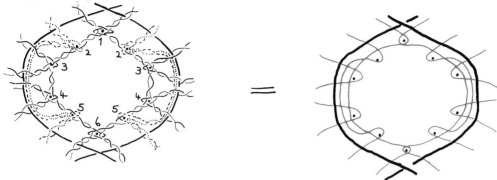

For an extra large honeycomb ring after the second pin on either side a pair is carried around with the gimp until needed at the fifth pin on both sides. The remainder is worked in the normal honeycomb manner.

Pinchain

A line of continuous honeycomb stitches creates a pinchain.

Gimps

Throughout the work always cross the gimps the same way.

Tying off gimps

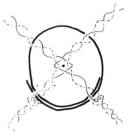

If possible always fold the two gimp ends over each other so that they may pass between at least four pairs.

In the event of it being impossible for the gimp ends to pass through more than two pairs it is advisable to tie each pair in order to secure the ends before cutting off the gimps.

Picot

Double-threaded picot on left-hand side

twist the pairs ×5

put pin on top of outside thread

    twist the pin clockwise so that the point of the pin takes the thread round with it, making a loop around the pin

pin up this loop in indicated pin hole

    with inner thread of the pair make another loop around the set pin also in a clockwise direction allowing this loop to fall under the first loop

twist pairs ×3

take care that the threads entwine around each other

for right-hand side picot the whole procedure is reversed.

Heading pairs

When making a heading there are usually one or two continuous pairs which remain on the outer edge – so making a smooth line. These pairs have only been drawn in the book for the first few centimetres so as to give a clear look to the diagrams – but they do continue for the full length of the piece.

BEES

Bobbins 13 pairs – **Gimps** 1 pair

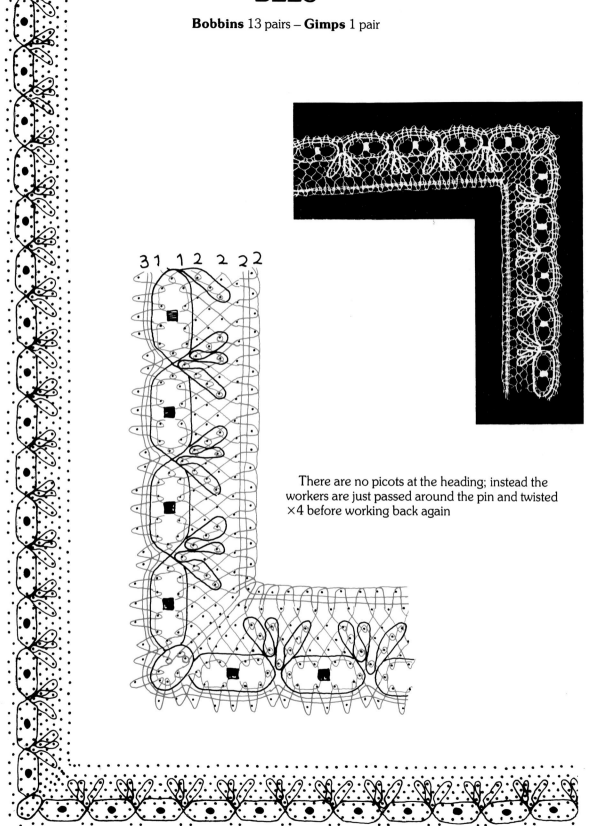

There are no picots at the heading; instead the
workers are just passed around the pin and twisted
×4 before working back again

RED ADMIRAL

Bobbins 14 pairs – **Gimps** 1 pair

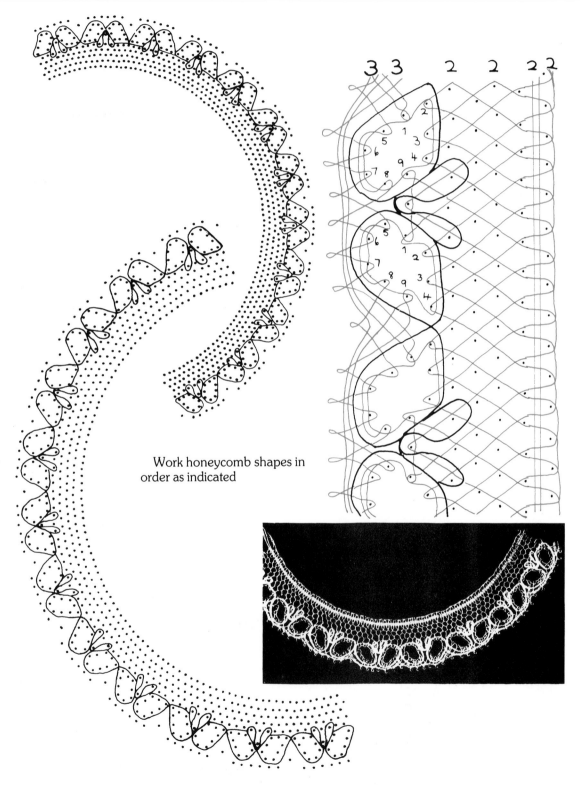

Work honeycomb shapes in
order as indicated

IVY

Bobbins 16 pairs – **Gimps** 1 continuous plus one pair for each repeat

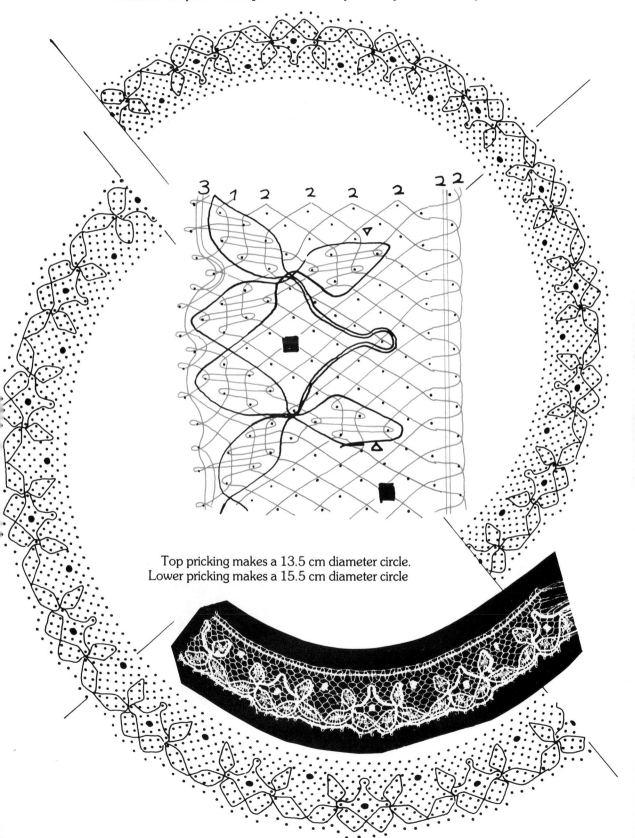

Top pricking makes a 13.5 cm diameter circle.
Lower pricking makes a 15.5 cm diameter circle

PAM

Bobbins 16 pairs – **Gimps** 1 pair

SAPPHIRES

Bobbins 15 pairs + 1 extra for corner – **Gimps** 1 pair

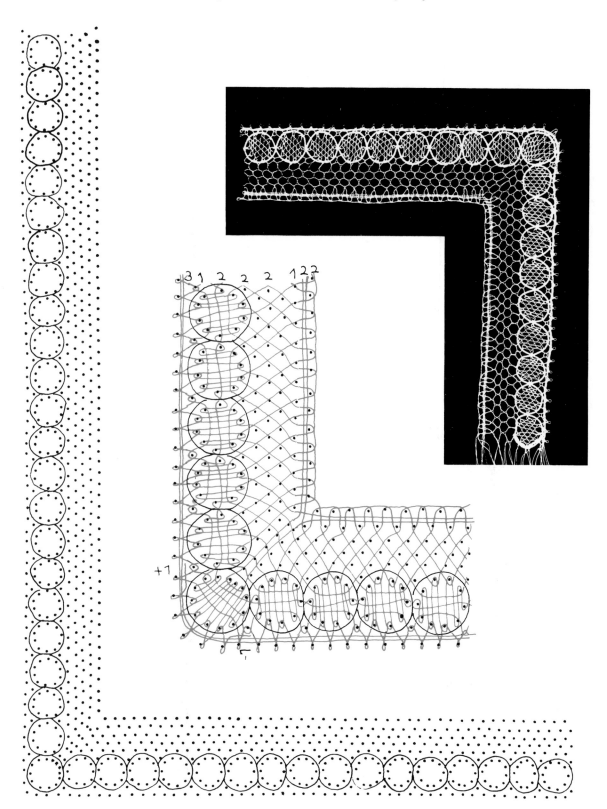

CORAL REEF

Bobbins 17 pairs – **Gimps** 1 pair + 2 single

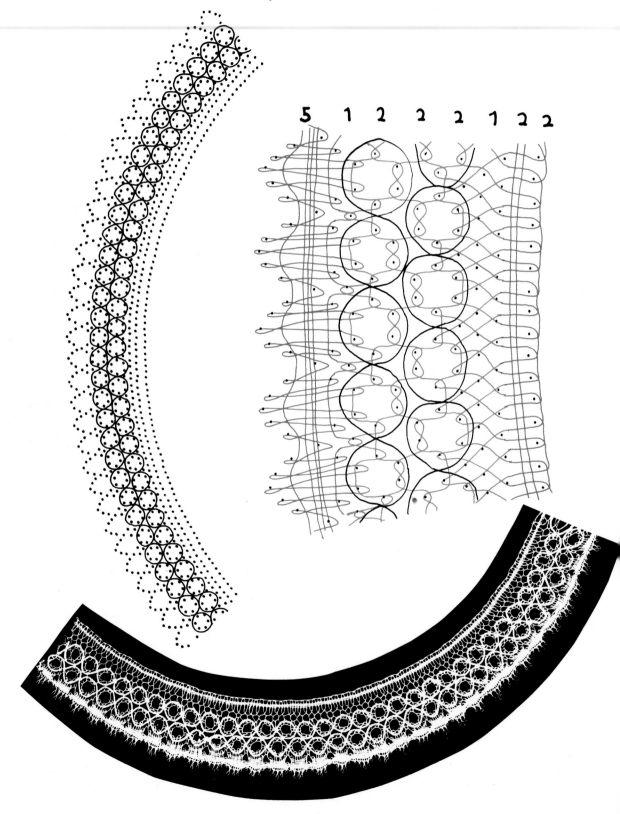

DIAMONDS

Bobbins 17 pairs

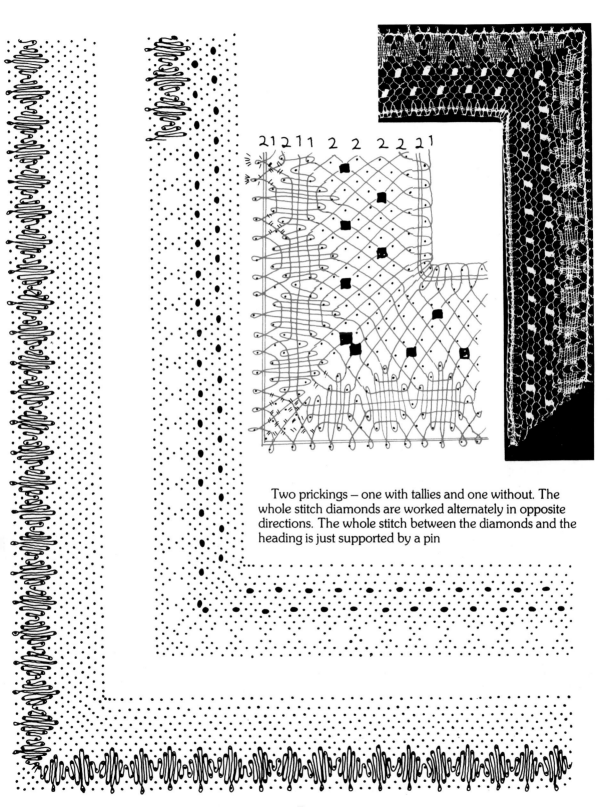

2 1 2 1 1 2 2 2 2 2 1 1

Two prickings – one with tallies and one without. The whole stitch diamonds are worked alternately in opposite directions. The whole stitch between the diamonds and the heading is just supported by a pin

MOUNTAINS

Bobbins 17 pairs + 1 extra pair at corner – **Gimps** 1 pair + 1 single

Weave gimp over and under individual pairs in both directions

BLUEBERRY

Bobbins 18 pairs + 2 extra pairs at corner – **Gimps** 1 pair

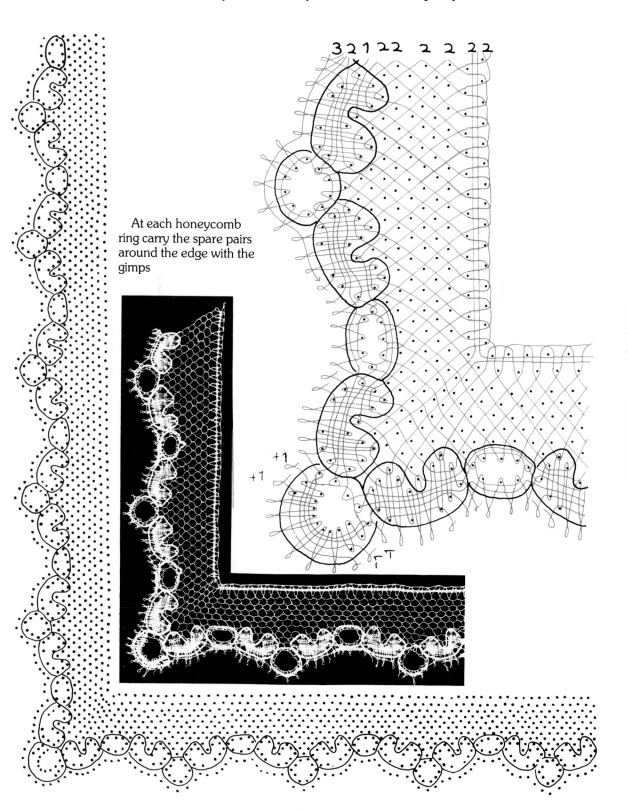

At each honeycomb ring carry the spare pairs around the edge with the gimps

9

CANTERBURY BELLS

Bobbins 18 pairs – **Gimps** 1 pair for each repeat + 2 pairs for corner motif

RIBBONS AND BOWS

Bobbins 18 pairs – **Gimps** 2 pairs + 1 single

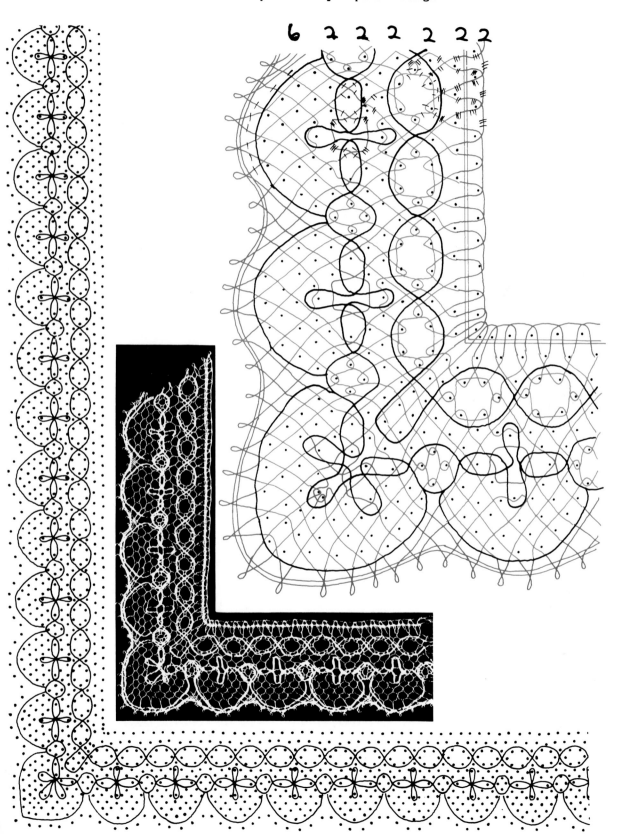

ENID

Bobbins 18 pairs –
Gimps 1 pair + 1 extra for corners

6 2 2 2 2 2 2

CLEMATIS

Bobbins 18 pairs – **Gimps** 1 pair + 3 single

Thirty-one repeats make a complete circle of each of the sizes shown

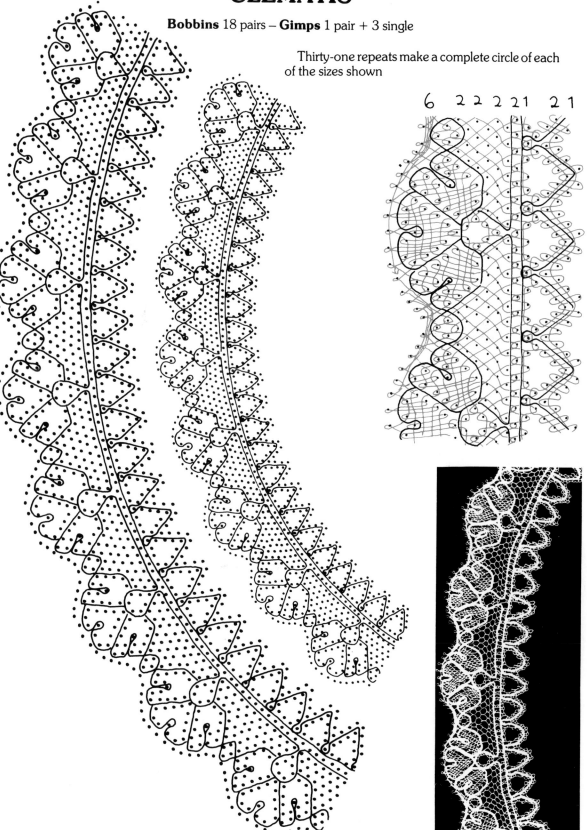

BIG FOOT

Bobbins 20 pairs – **Gimps** 1 pair

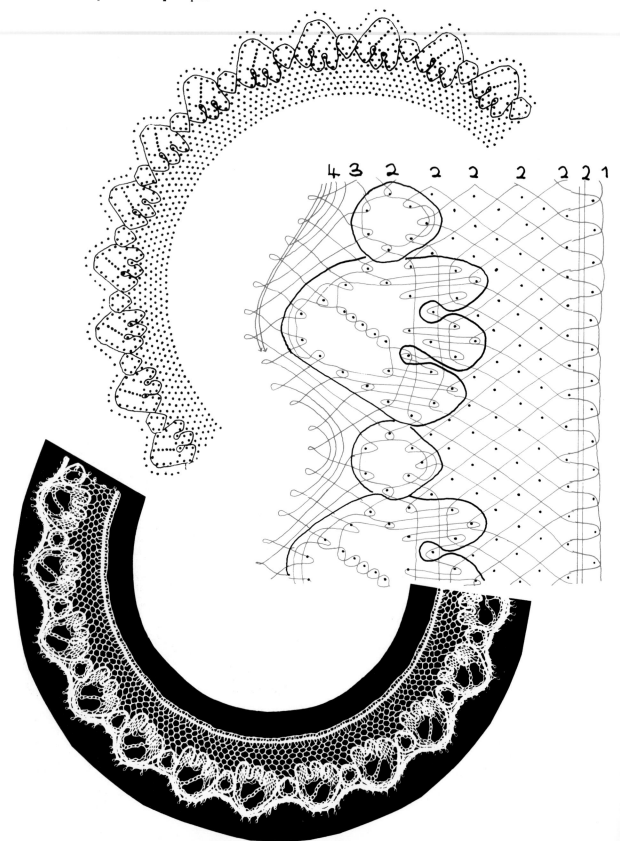

RICHARD

Bobbins 20 pairs – **Gimps** 2 single

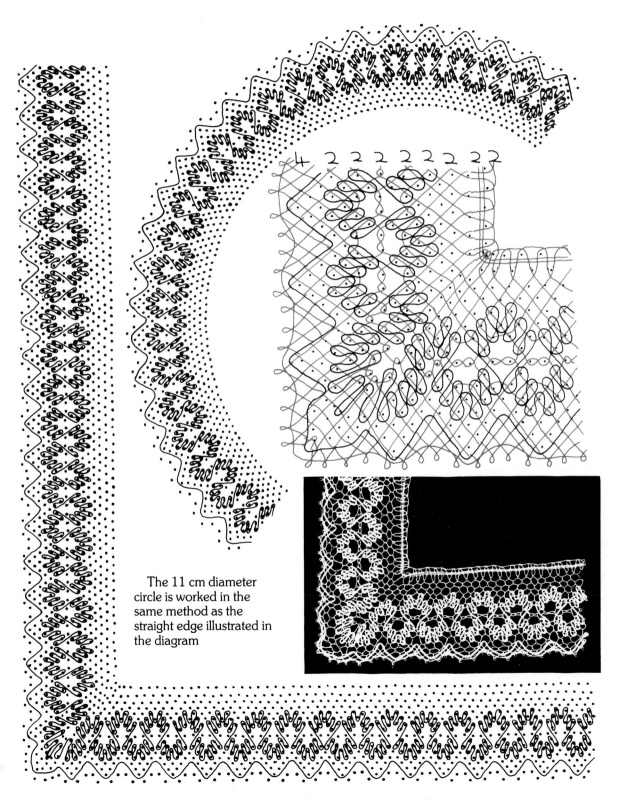

4 2 2 2 2 2 2 2 2

The 11 cm diameter circle is worked in the same method as the straight edge illustrated in the diagram

ASTERS

Bobbins 20 pairs – **Gimps** 1 pair + 1 single

Six sections complete a circle. Three different sizes are shown here

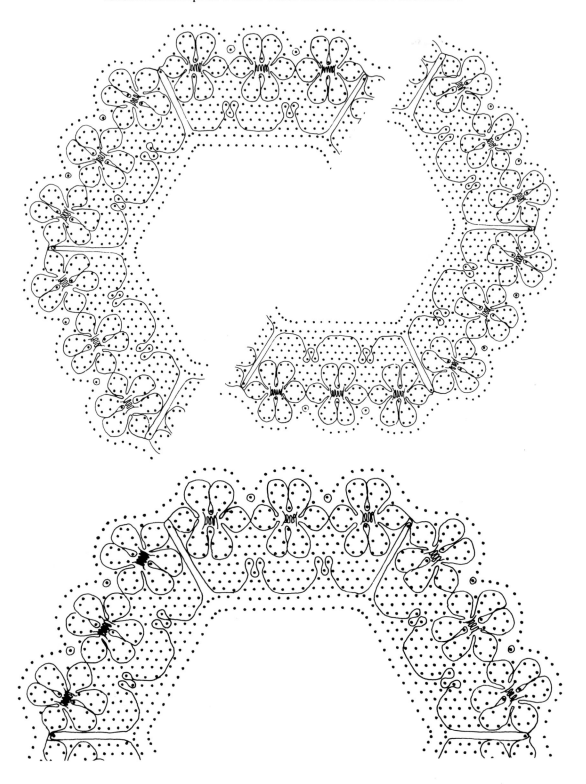

ASTERS

Bobbins 20 pairs – **Gimps** 1 pair + 1 single

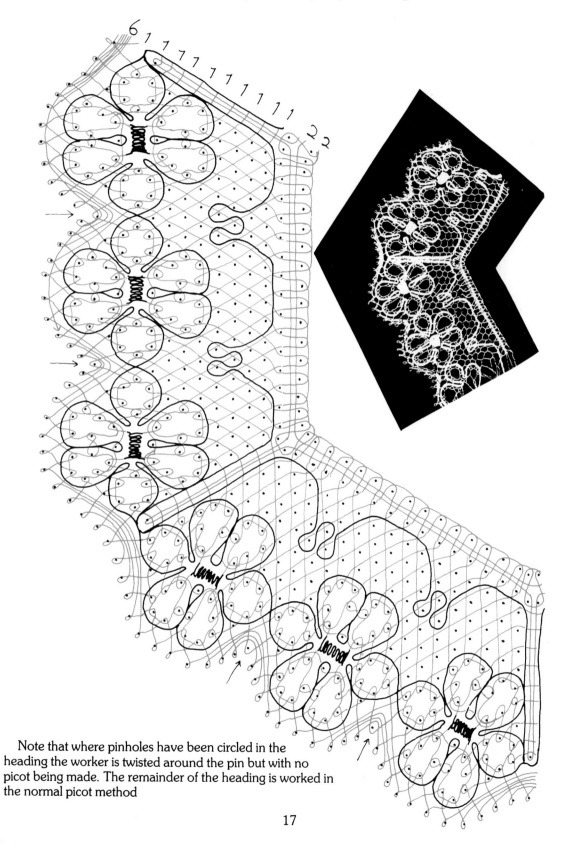

Note that where pinholes have been circled in the heading the worker is twisted around the pin but with no picot being made. The remainder of the heading is worked in the normal picot method

NICHOLAS

Bobbins 21 pairs – **Gimps** 1 pair + 1 single

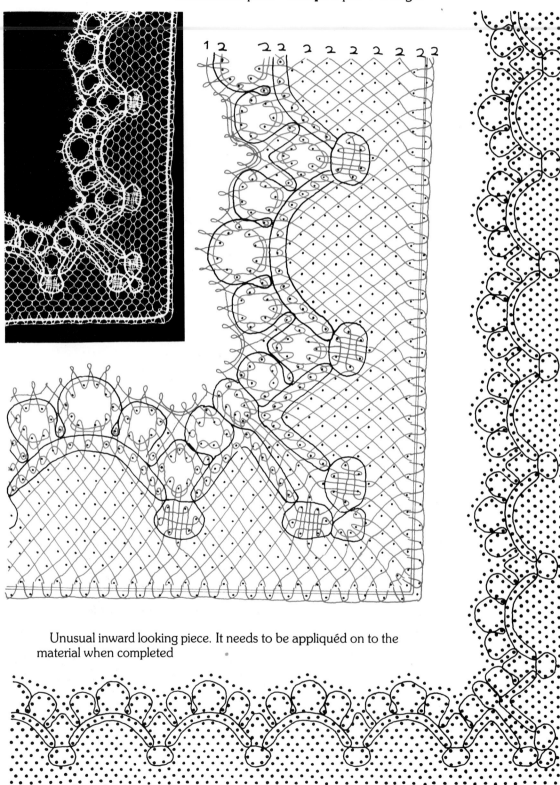

Unusual inward looking piece. It needs to be appliquéd on to the material when completed

STARFISH

Bobbins 21 pairs – **Gimps** 2 pairs + 1 single

19

NORTH STAR

Bobbins 21 pairs – **Gimps** 1 pair

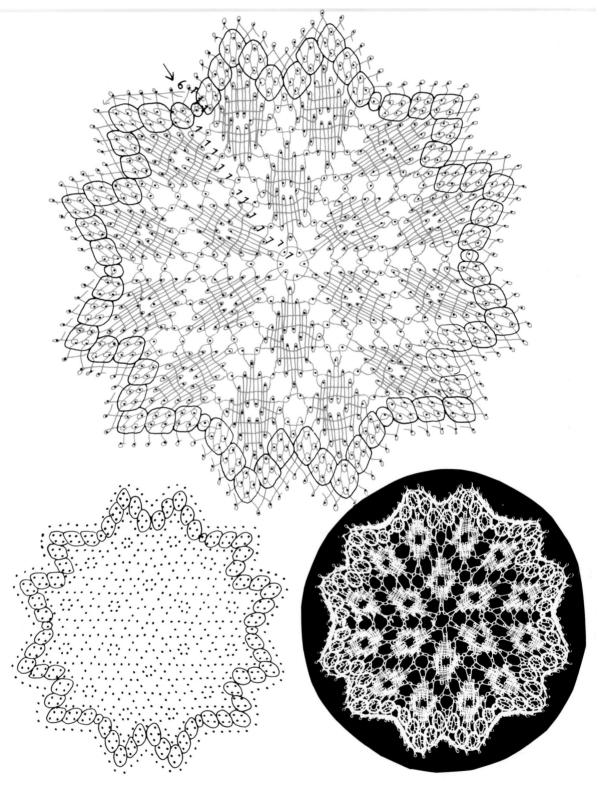

ETERNITY RINGS

Bobbins 21 pairs – **Gimps** 3 pairs

RINGS AND HEARTS

Bobbins 21 pairs – **Gimps** 2 pairs + 1 single (for centre)

22

FORGET-ME-NOT

Bobbins 22 pairs – **Gimps** 1 pair

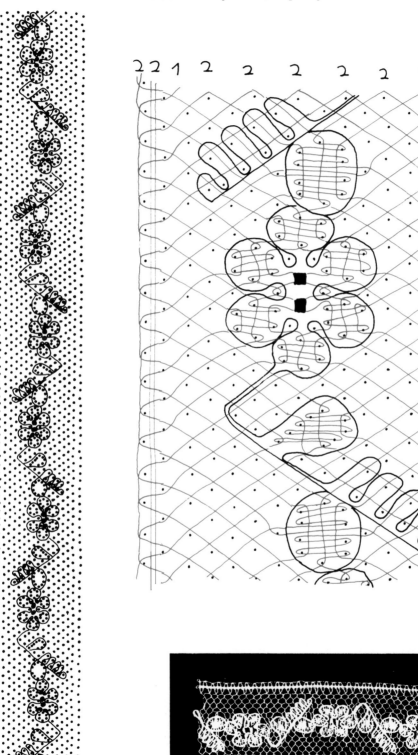

HOLLY BERRIES

Bobbins 22 pairs – **Gimps** 1 pair

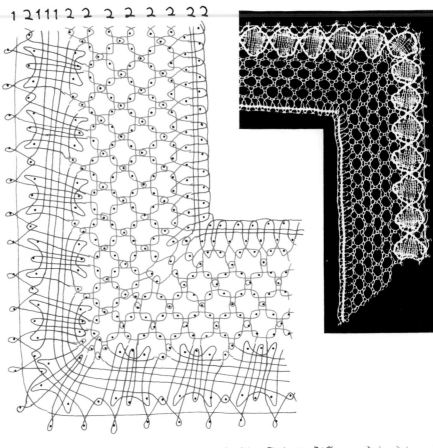

1 21112 2 2 2 2 2 2 22

The first worker pair is worked across the bud. At the edge it is supported by a pin before passing the gimp through it. The pair is then twisted once, and the gimp is passed back through that pair which now hang down and become a passive pair. A new worker pair is then taken in and worked in accordance with the diagram

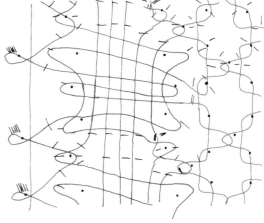

24

JENNIFER

Bobbins 23 pairs – **Gimps** 1 single

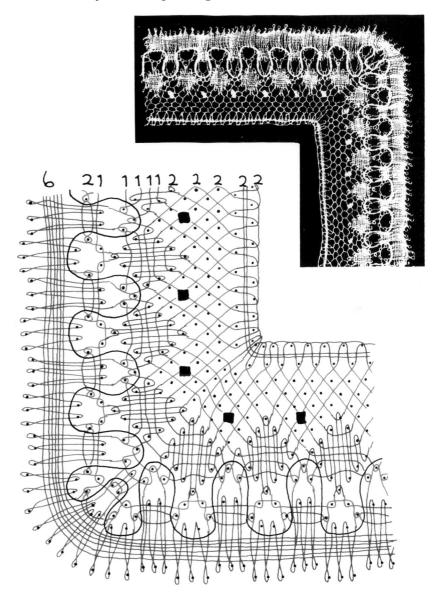

The worker that whole stitches the outer edge changes at a honey comb stitch after working 3 picots

PANSY

Bobbins 23 pairs – **Gimps** 2 pairs

EILEEN

Bobbins 23 pairs – **Gimps** 1 pair + 1 single

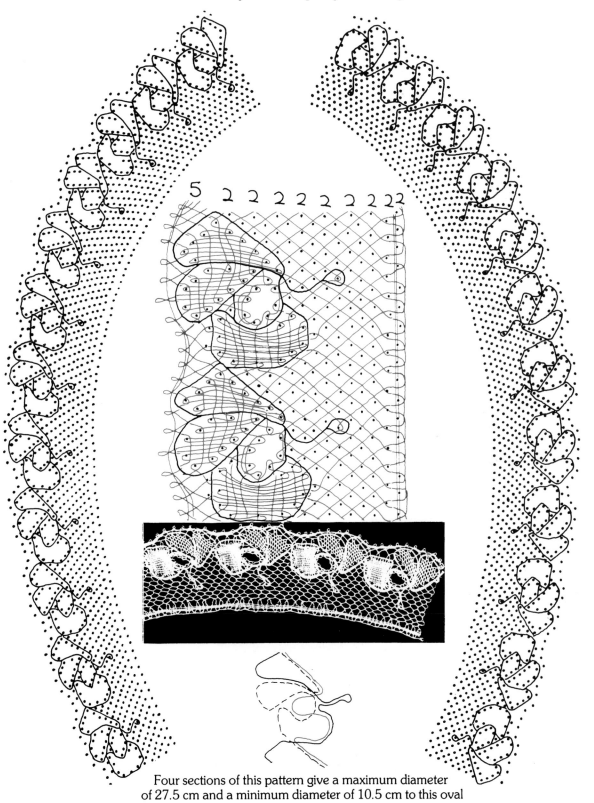

Four sections of this pattern give a maximum diameter
of 27.5 cm and a minimum diameter of 10.5 cm to this oval

MARIA

Bobbins 23 pairs – **Gimps** 2 pairs

LENA

Bobbins 24 pairs – **Gimps** 2 pairs

BURNING BUSH

Bobbins 24 pairs – **Gimps** 1 pair + 1 single

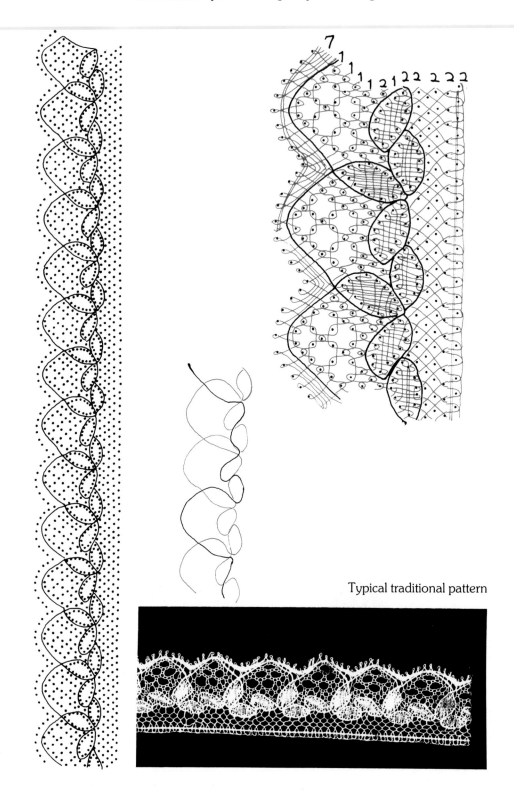

7
7
1
1
1
1 2 1 2 2 2 2 2 2

Typical traditional pattern

JULIE

Bobbins 24 pairs

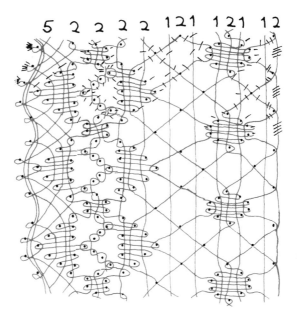

This pattern consists of French Ground or Kat stitch which is worked entirely in whole stitch

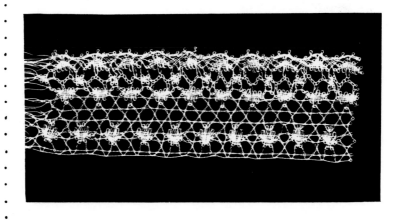

31

CAMPANULA

Bobbins 25 pairs + 5 pairs for corner – **Gimps** 2 pairs

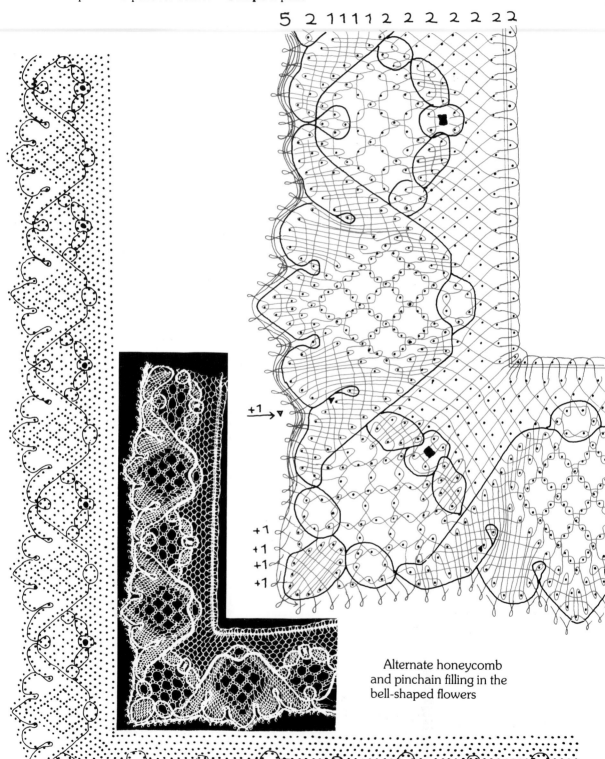

5 2 1 1 1 1 2 2 2 2 2 2 2

+1 → ▽

+1
+1
+1
+1

Alternate honeycomb
and pinchain filling in the
bell-shaped flowers

WHEAT EARS

Bobbins 26 pairs – **Gimps** 1 pair

STEVEN

Bobbins 26 pairs – **Gimps** 2 pairs + 1 extra pair for each flower repeat

CHAIN LINK

Bobbins 27 pairs – **Gimps** 2 pairs + 1 extra at corner

On reaching a corner the passives are used in the heading, and when the corner is turned they are taken back into the work as passives

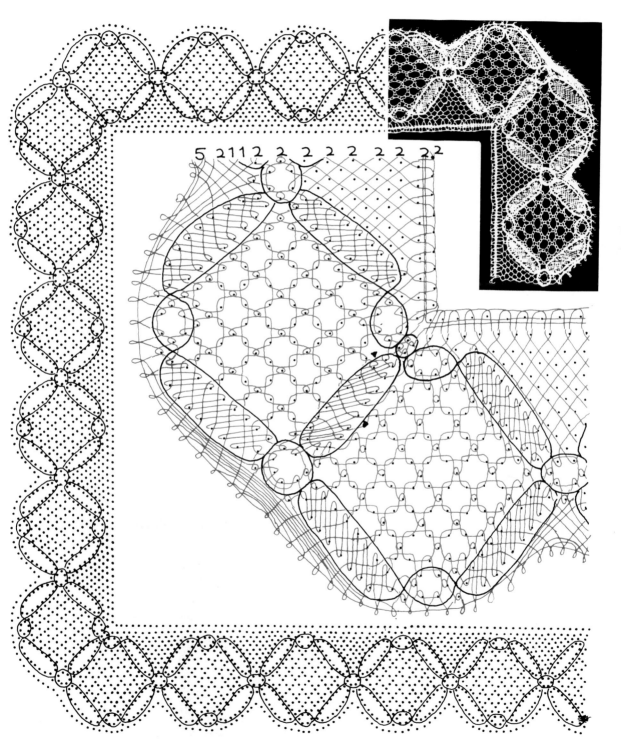

5 2 1 1 2 2 2 2 2 2 2 2

LUCKY CLOVER

Bobbins 27 pairs – **Gimps** 1 pair + 2 singles

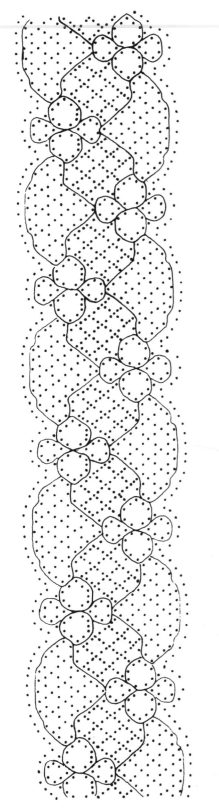

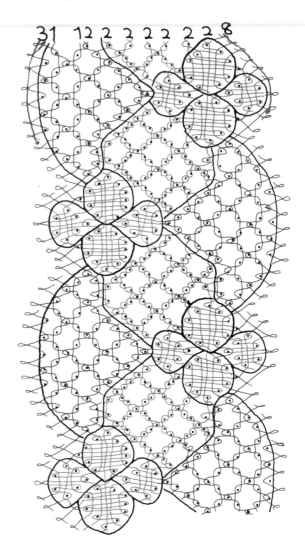

Double-sided insertion

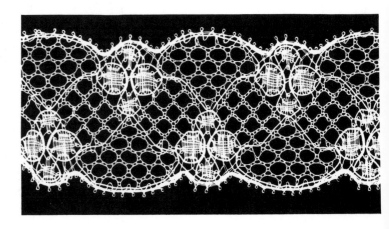

STEPPING STONES

Bobbins 27 pairs – **Gimps** 1 pair + 1 single

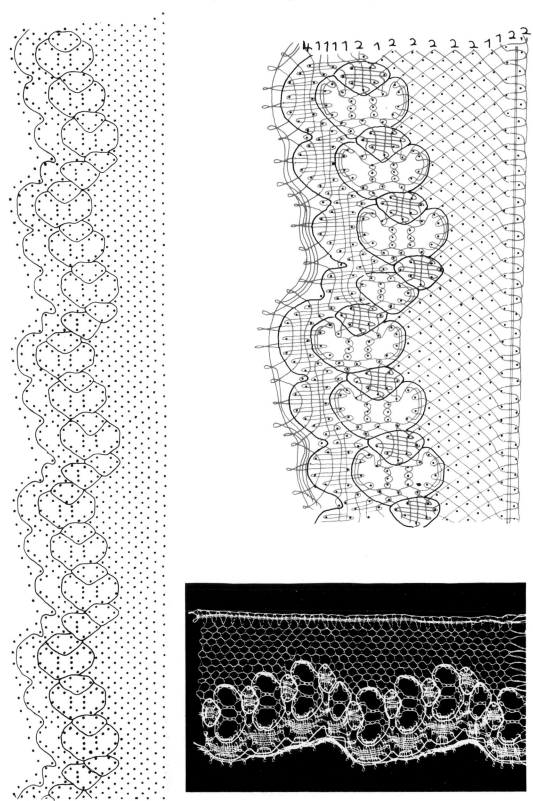

37

ORANGE BLOSSOM

Bobbins 28 pairs – **Gimps** 3 pairs

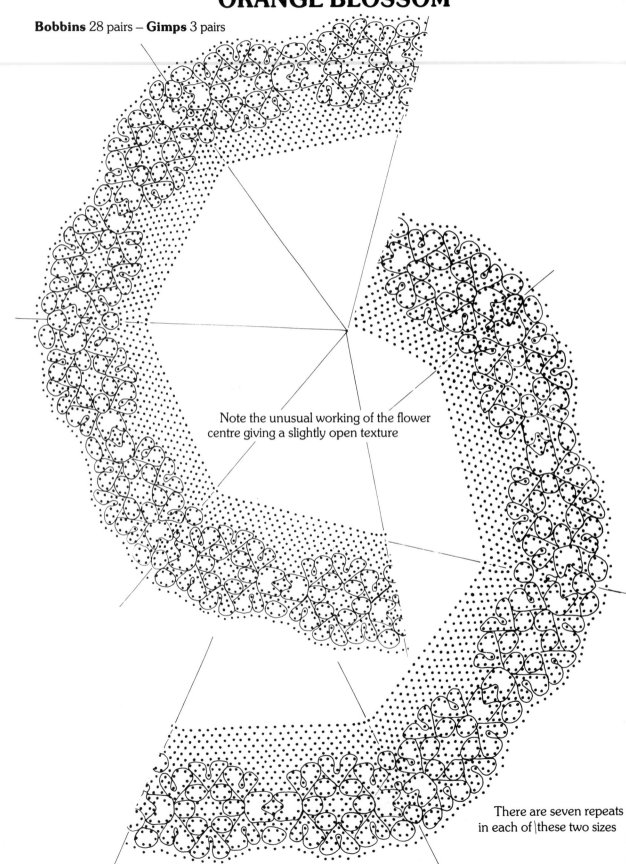

Note the unusual working of the flower
centre giving a slightly open texture

There are seven repeats
in each of \these two sizes

ORANGE BLOSSOM

Bobbins 28 pairs – **Gimps** 3 pairs

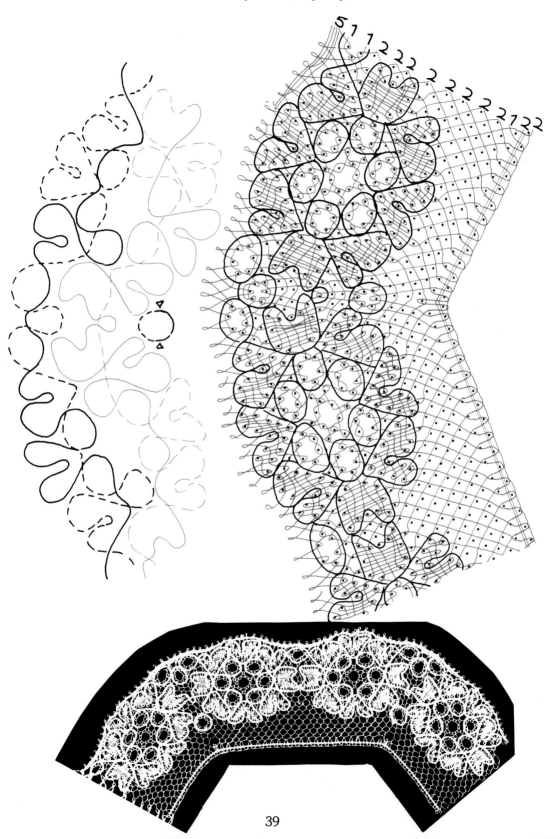

HAREBELLS

Bobbins 29 pairs – **Gimps** 2 pairs

HAREBELLS

Bobbins 29 pairs – **Gimps** 2 pairs

The pinchain flower centres are
made with three continuous
honeycomb stitches

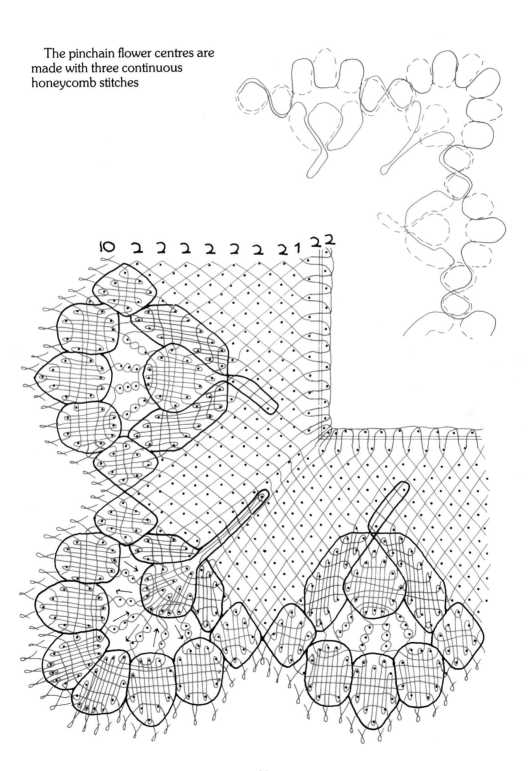

GERRY

Bobbins 29 pairs – **Gimps** 2 pairs

Horsehoe shaped collar back

GERRY

Bobbins 29 pairs – **Gimps** 2 pairs

Horseshoe shaped collar sides

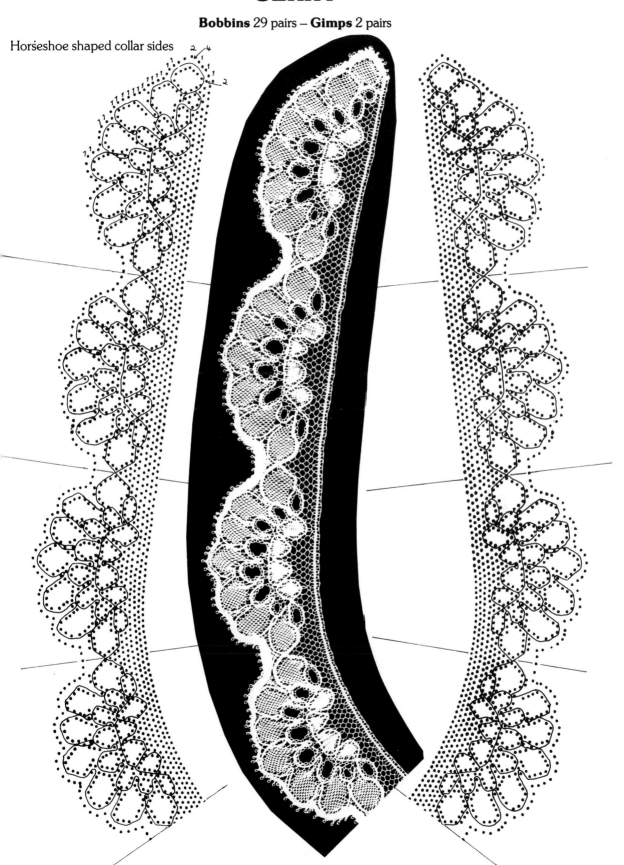

CAMERA EYE

Bobbins 29 pairs – **Gimps** 3 single + 1 new pair in each pattern repeat

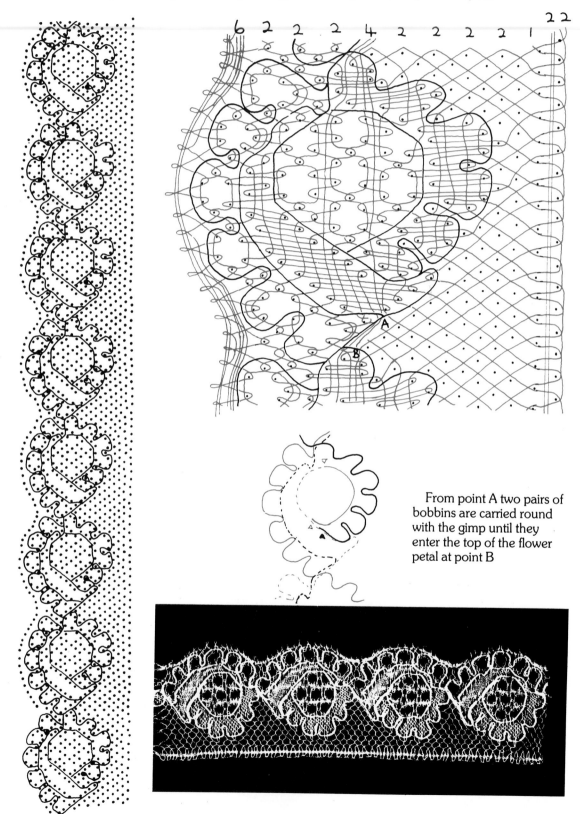

From point A two pairs of bobbins are carried round with the gimp until they enter the top of the flower petal at point B

44

SUNRISE

Bobbins 29 pairs – **Gimps** 2 pairs

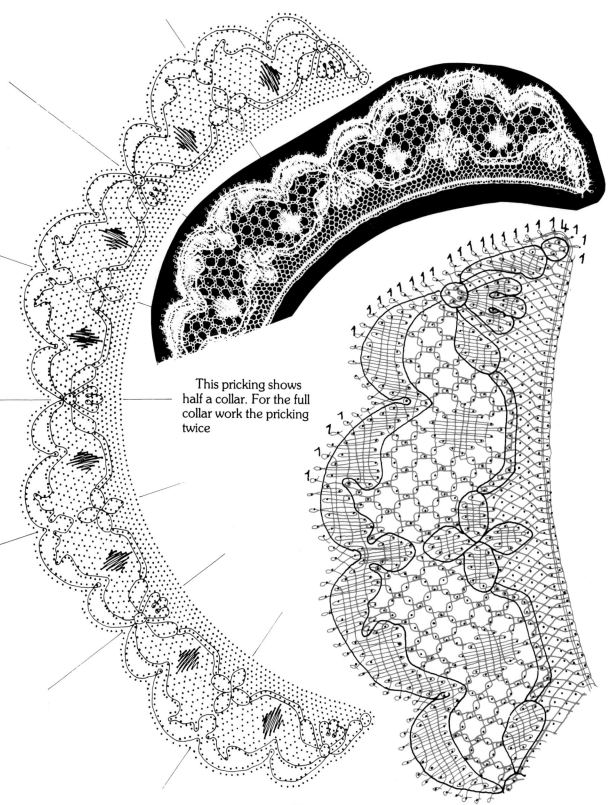

This pricking shows
half a collar. For the full
collar work the pricking
twice

DOROTHY

Bobbins 30 pairs – **Gimps** 1 single

ANNA

Bobbins 30 pairs – **Gimps** 2 pairs

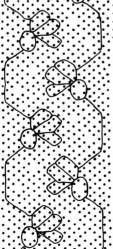

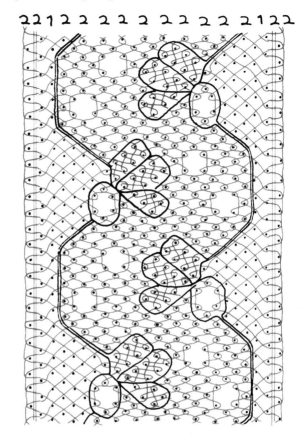

An insertion – with the honeycomb stitch
used in an unusual way

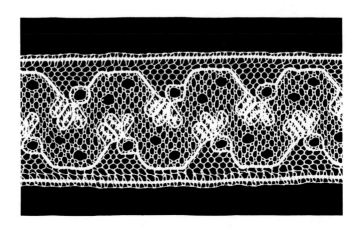

FLORAL DOMINO

Bobbins 30 pairs – **Gimps** 1 single for edge, 2 pairs for each flower repeat

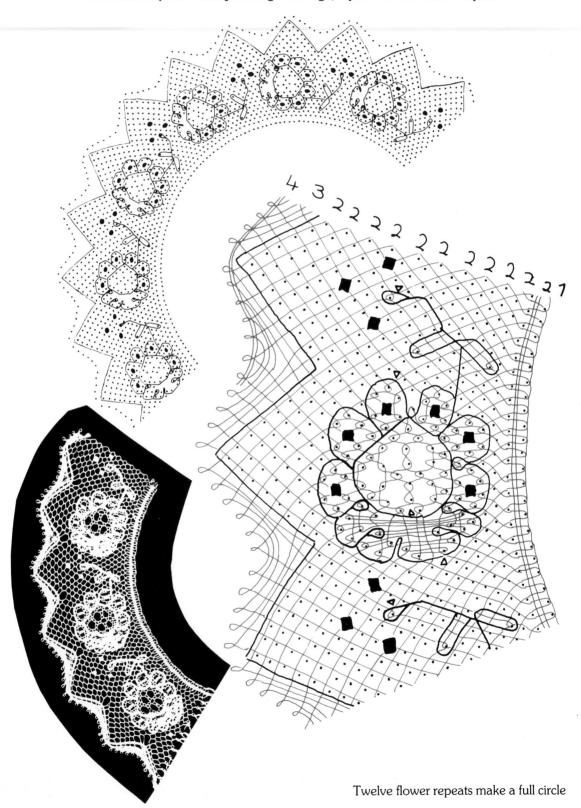

Twelve flower repeats make a full circle

SHARK'S TOOTH

Bobbins 32 pairs – **Gimps** 3 pairs

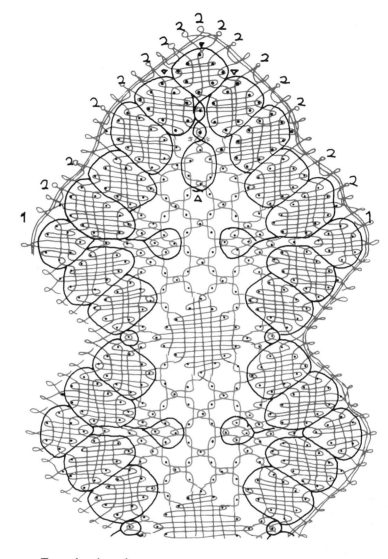

Tie or bookmark
   Section BC can be repeated until the required length is reached.
Finish with section AB reversed

COLLAR OF LILY

Bobbins 32 pairs and 2 pairs for each repeat until center of collar, 45 pairs in all –
Gimps 4 pairs. 2 pairs ending at each repeat and 2 new pairs at each new pattern

Right- and left-hand sides of shaped collar

COLLAR OF LILY

Bobbins 32 pairs and 2 pairs for each repeat until centre of collar, 45 pairs in all –
Gimps 4 pairs. 2 pairs ending at each repeat and 2 new pairs at each new pattern

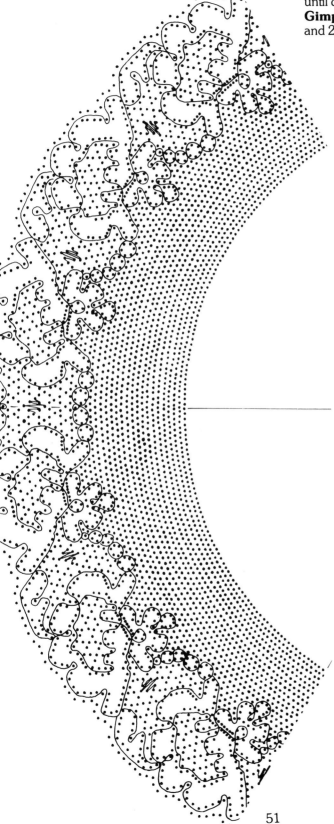

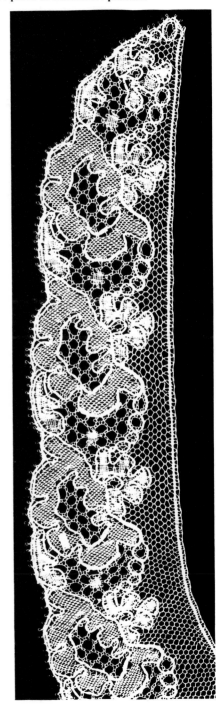

Back section of shaped collar

COLLAR OF LILY

Bobbins 32 pairs and 2 pairs for each repeat until centre of collar, 45 pairs in all –
Gimps 4 pairs. 2 pairs ending at each repeat and 2 new pairs at each new pattern

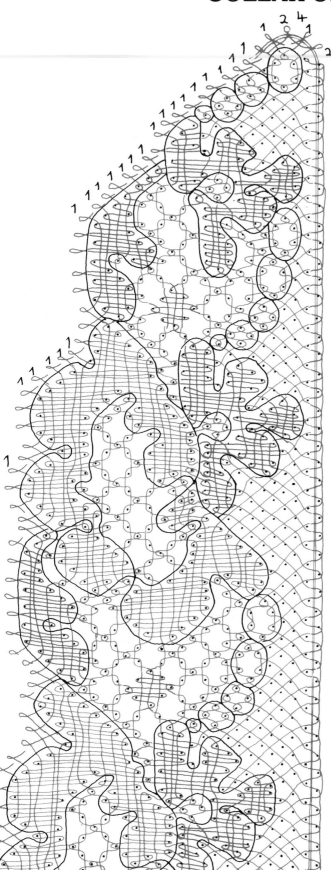

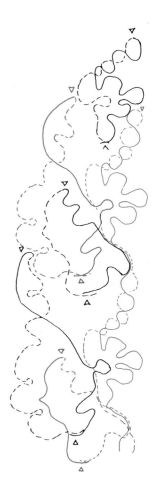

This collar is quite interesting as the net increases at the back of the neck so draping well on the garment

SARAH

Bobbins 33 pairs – **Gimps** 1 pair + 1 single + 2 extra pairs for corner

5 1 2 12 2 2 2 2 2 2 2 2 2 22

CRYSTAL CUFF

Bobbins 33 pairs – **Gimps** 2 pairs

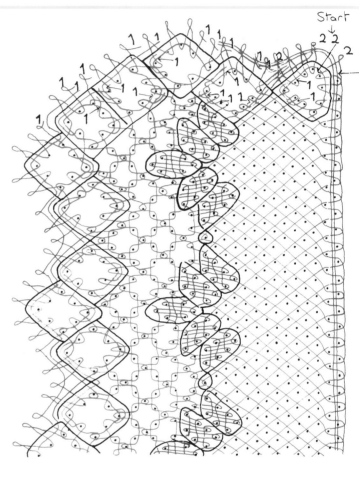

Work the edge of honeycomb squares from the footside to
the picot heading. Then turn work and continue in the normal
way. At the end work in reverse as for start

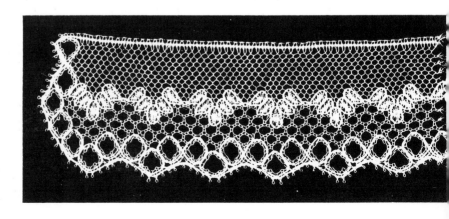

CRYSTAL COLLAR

Bobbins 33 pairs – **Gimps** 2 pairs

Start at inner corner and work honeycomb squares first, then turn work and work down in the normal way

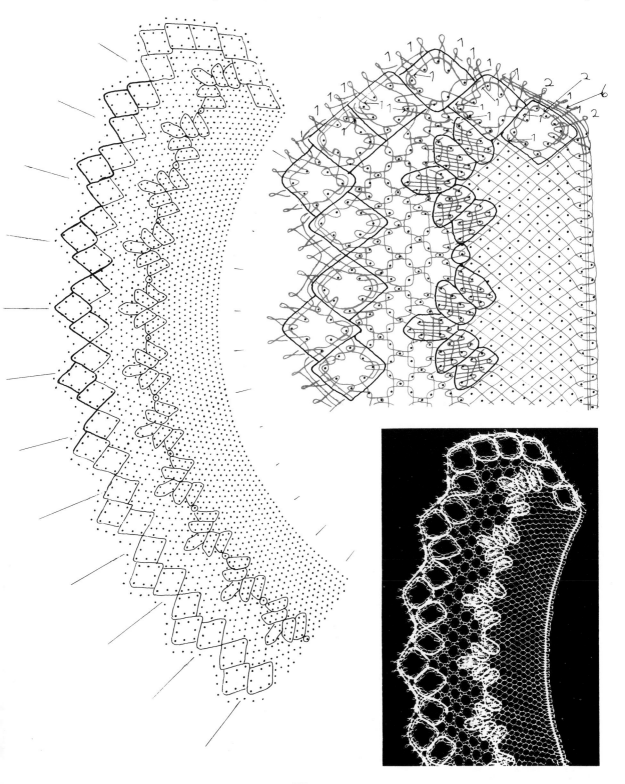

ORCHIDS

Bobbins 34 pairs – **Gimps** 3 pairs for flower + 1 single for edge + 1 extra pair for corner

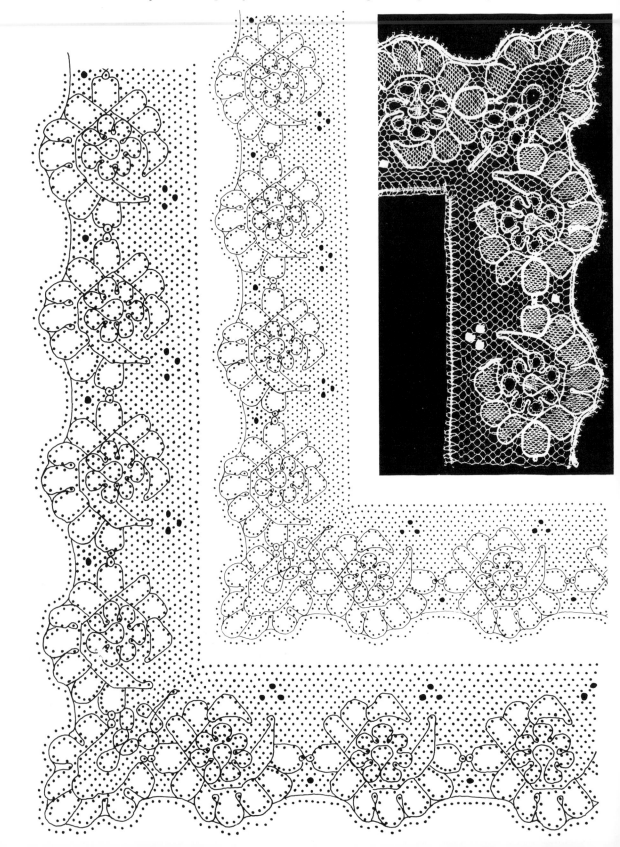

ORCHIDS

Bobbins 34 pairs – **Gimps** 3 pairs for flower + 1 single for edge + 1 extra pair for corner

The pattern is not reversed at the corner but is worked in the same direction after the corner has been turned

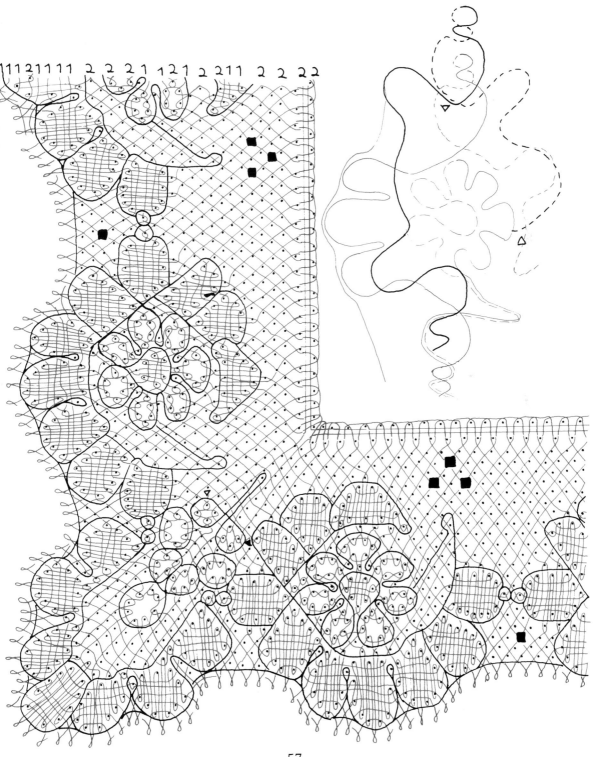

57

DOMINO ONE

Bobbins 34 pairs – **Gimps** 3 pairs + 1 pair for each spot

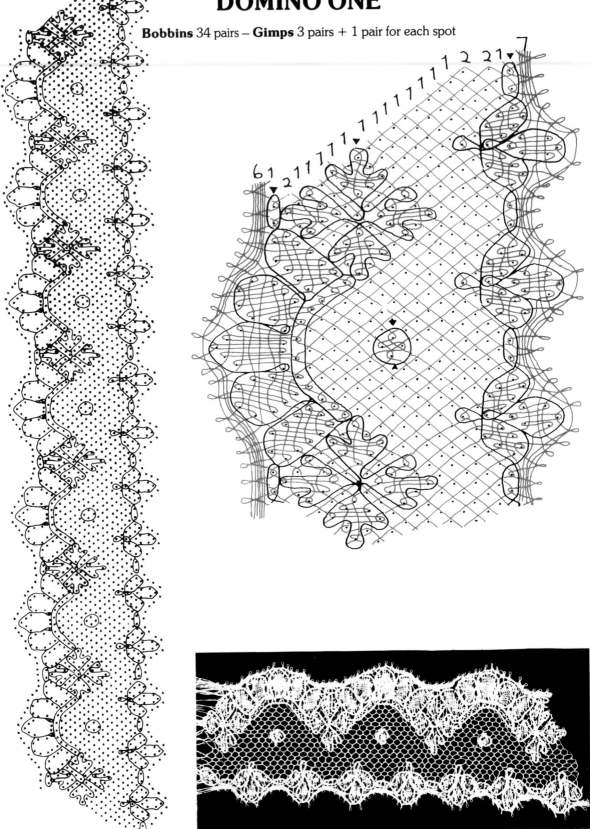

GERANIUM

Bobbins 35 pairs – **Gimps** 2 pairs for each repeat

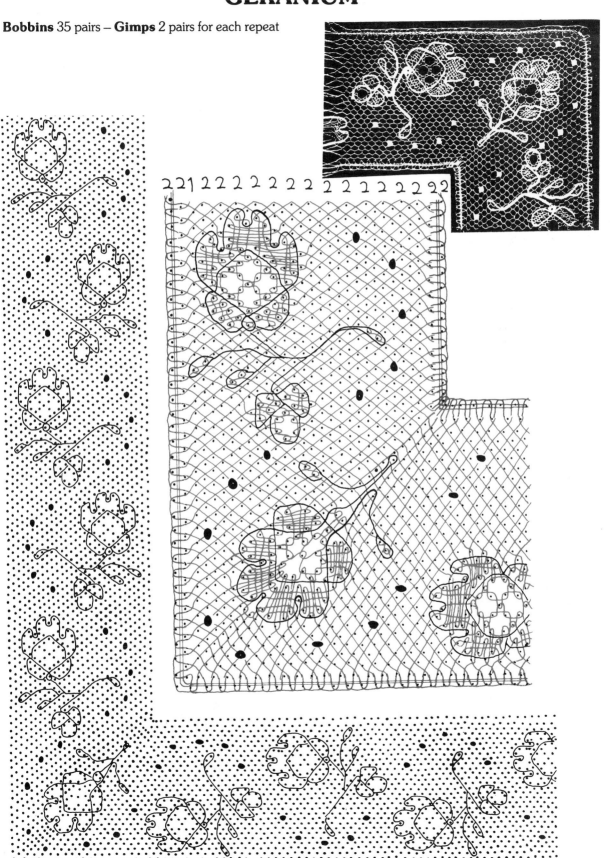

LOVE GARTER

Bobbins 36 pairs – **Gimps** 5 pairs

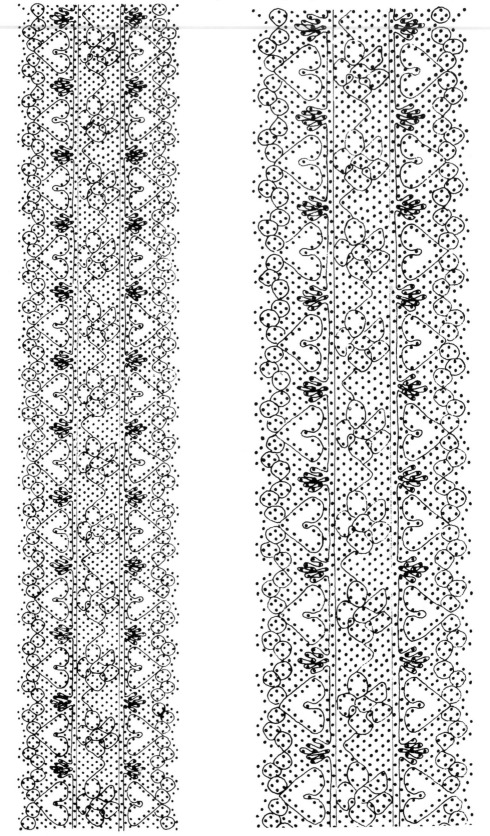

LOVE GARTER

Bobbins 36 pairs – **Gimps** 5 pairs

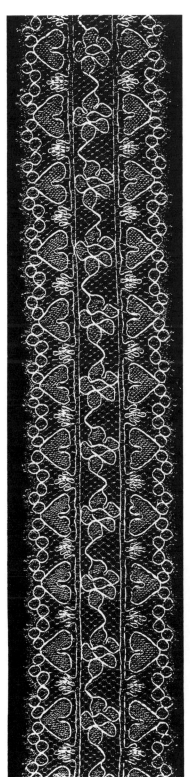

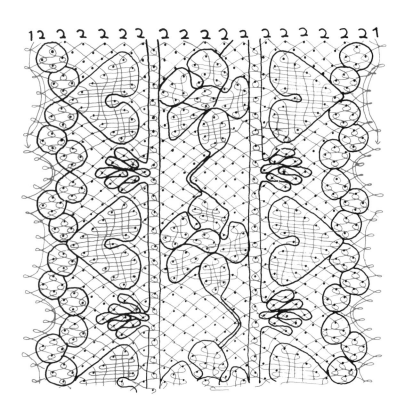

66 cm will make an attractive wedding garter. This one was made in blue and silver. Sew elastic behind the middle section only and gather in to the appropriate size

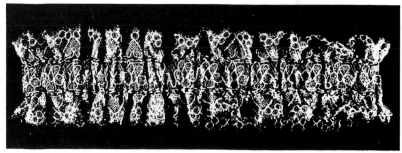

BUSY LIZZIE

Bobbins 36 pairs – **Gimps** 3 pairs

The pattern is not reversed at the corner but is worked in the same direction after the corner has been turned

BUSY LISSIE

Bobbins 36 pairs – **Gimps** 3 pairs

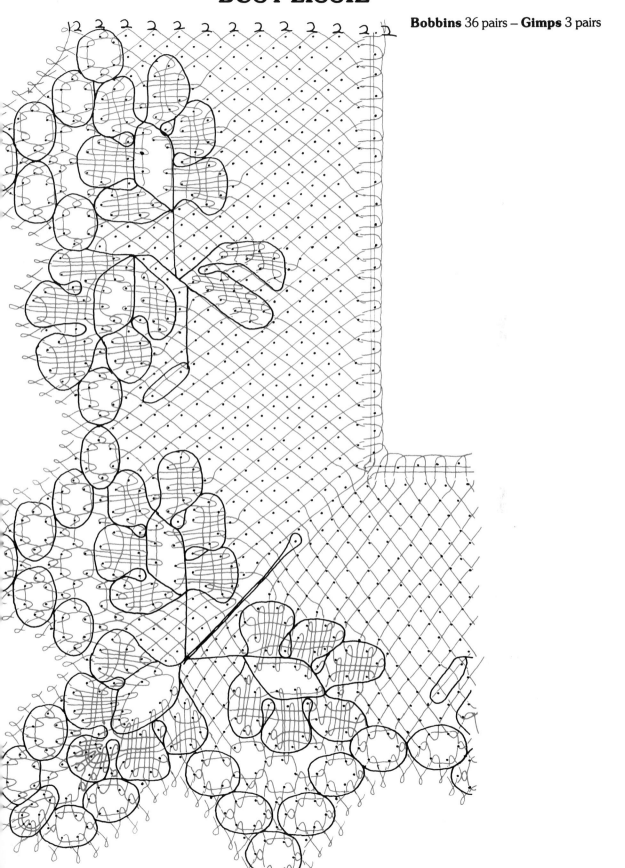

FLOWER BORDER

Bobbins 36 pairs – **Gimps** 2 pairs

FLOWER BORDER

Bobbins 36 pairs – **Gimps** 2 pairs

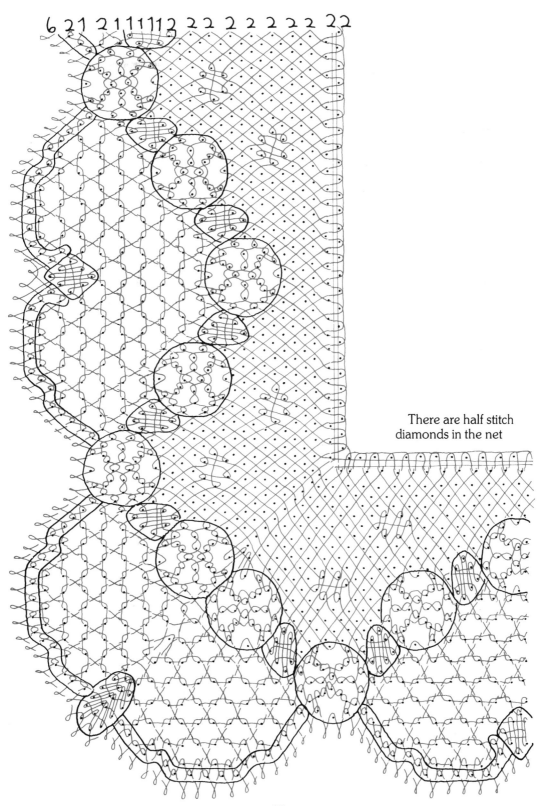

There are half stitch diamonds in the net

STRAWBERRY DELIGHT

Bobbins 38 pairs – **Gimps** 5 single

4 sections make a 17 cm diameter circle

In the honeycomb ring work pin A first – then work adjacent
pins and carry spare pairs around with the gimp

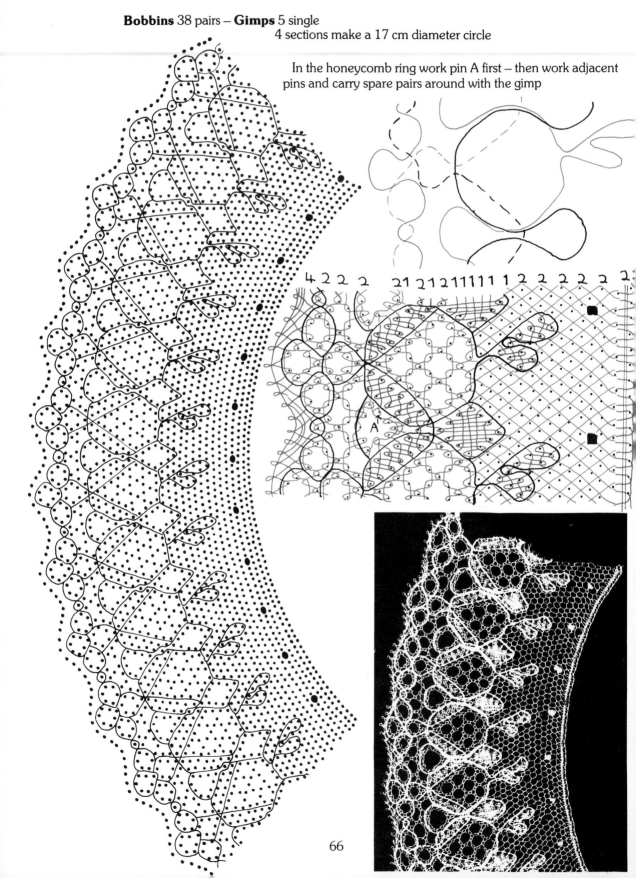

CHAMOMILE

Bobbins 40 pairs – **Gimps** 3 pairs

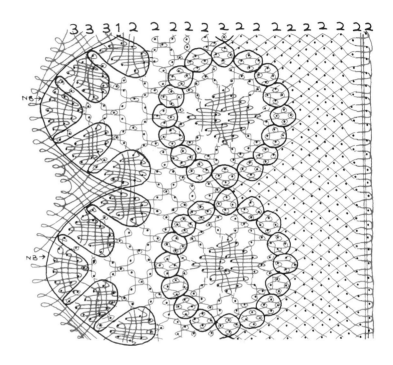

Note the change of workers in the central area of the top leaf

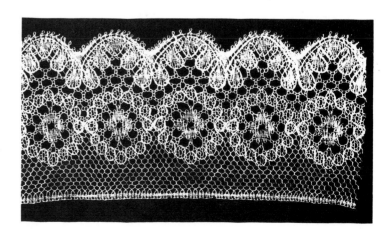

67

SURF

Bobbins 41 pairs + 6 extra for corner – **Gimps** 2 pairs + 1 extra for corner

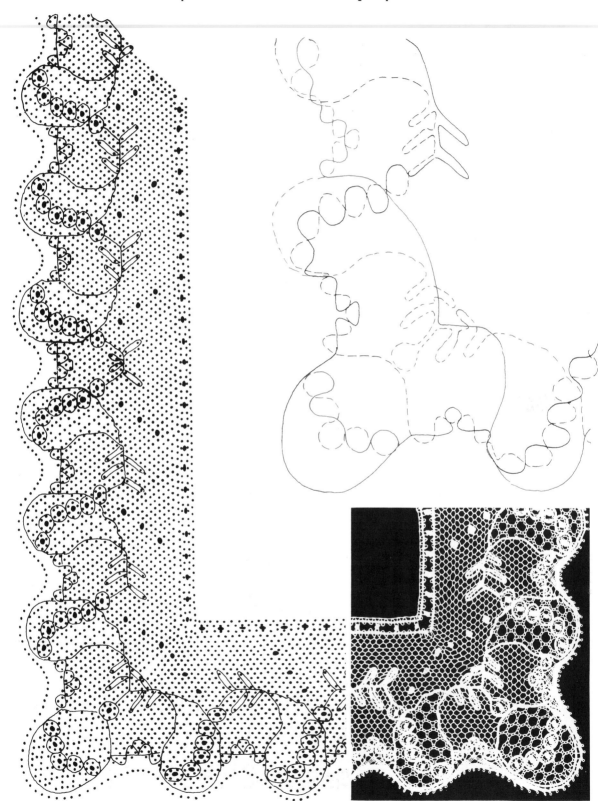

SURF

Bobbins 41 pairs + 6 extra for corner – **Gimps** 2 pairs + 1 extra for corner

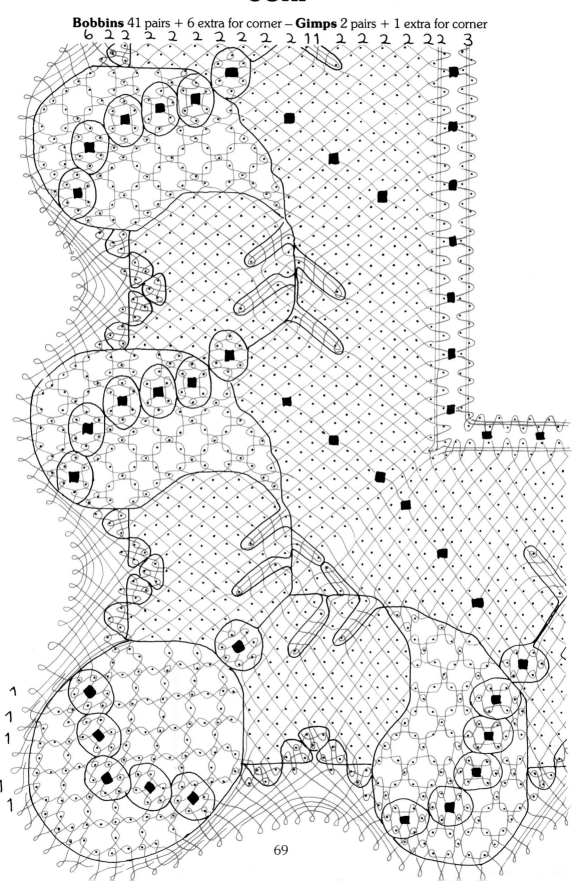

69

LOBELIA

Bobbins 42 pairs – **Gimps** 2 pairs for outer edge
1 pair for flowers
1 pair for leaves

The spots worked in the net are not gimped. Although worked sideways, the leaves of the motif are at the bottom

70

FLOWER PETALS

Bobbins 42 pairs – **Gimps** 2 pairs for edge
+ 3 pairs for flower motif

71

ICE TOPPING

Bobbins 42 pairs – **Gimps** 2 continuous pairs for main pattern
+ 1 pair for each flower repeat
+ 2 pairs in the outer edge to interchange with each other

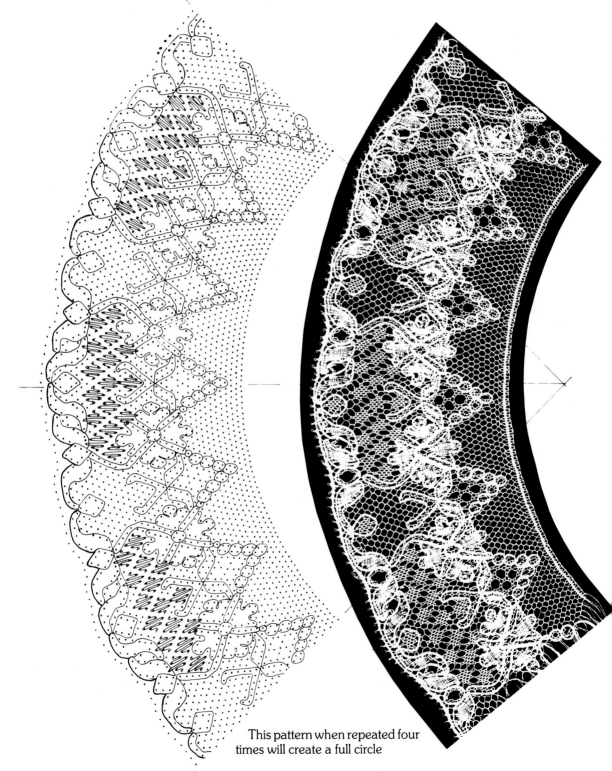

This pattern when repeated four
times will create a full circle

ICE TOPPING

Bobbins 42 pairs – **Gimps** 2 continuous pairs for main pattern
+ 1 pair for each flower repeat
+ 2 pairs in the outer edge to interchange with each other

JUGGLER

Bobbins 43 pairs – **Gimps** 4 pairs

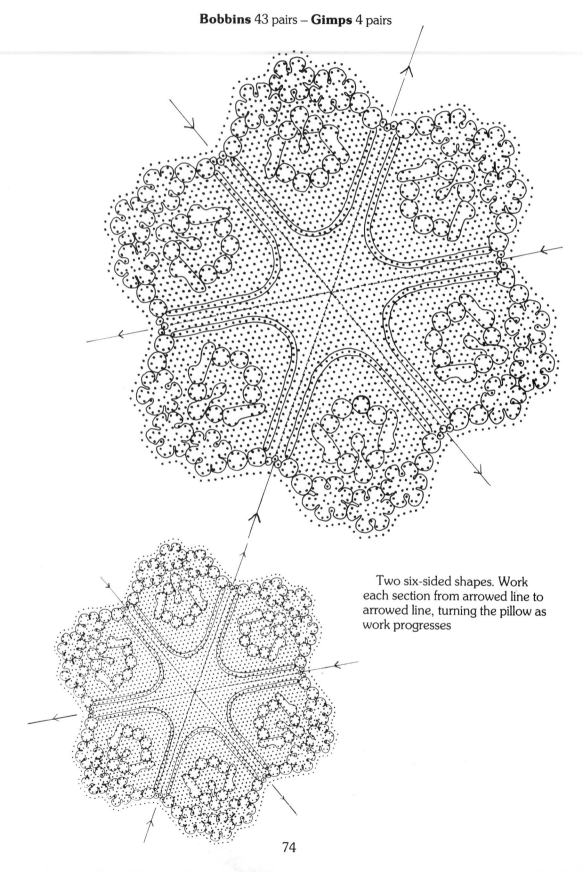

Two six-sided shapes. Work
each section from arrowed line to
arrowed line, turning the pillow as
work progresses

74

JUGGLER

Bobbins 43 pairs – **Gimps** 4 pairs

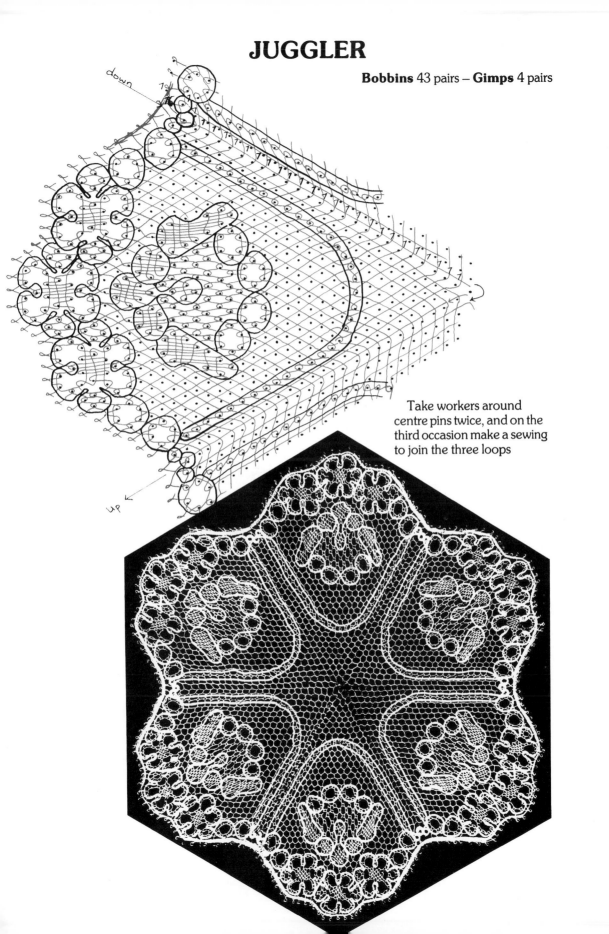

Take workers around
centre pins twice, and on the
third occasion make a sewing
to join the three loops

DI

Bobbins 43 pairs – **Gimps** 3 pairs
+ 1 extra pair for each flower repeat

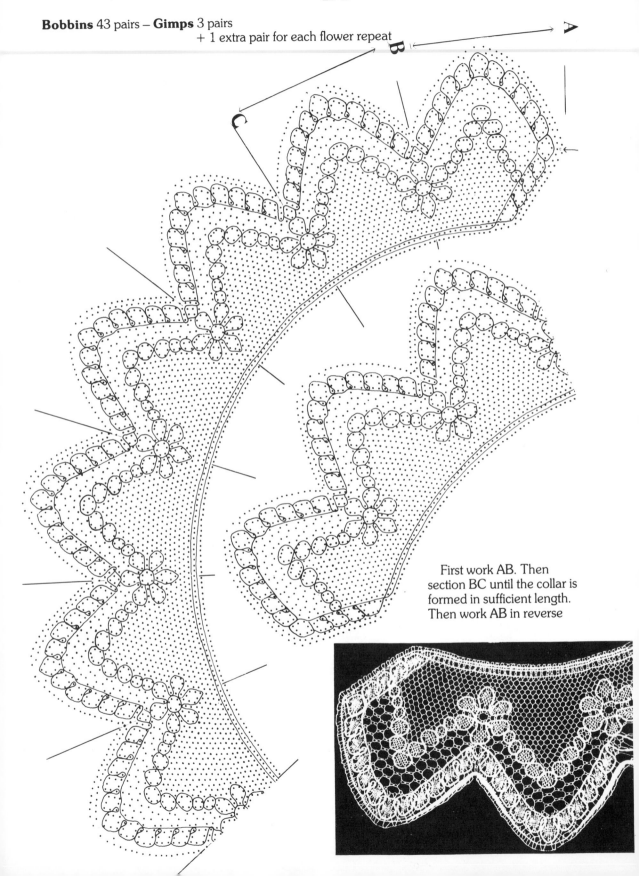

First work AB. Then section BC until the collar is formed in sufficient length. Then work AB in reverse

DI

Bobbins 43 pairs – **Gimps** 3 pairs
+ 1 extra pair for each flower repeat

In the outer edge the passive
pairs are passed between the
workers in the gimp manner –
bunched together. This makes
a neat rolled edge. New pairs
are taken in or out of the bunch
as and when needed for use

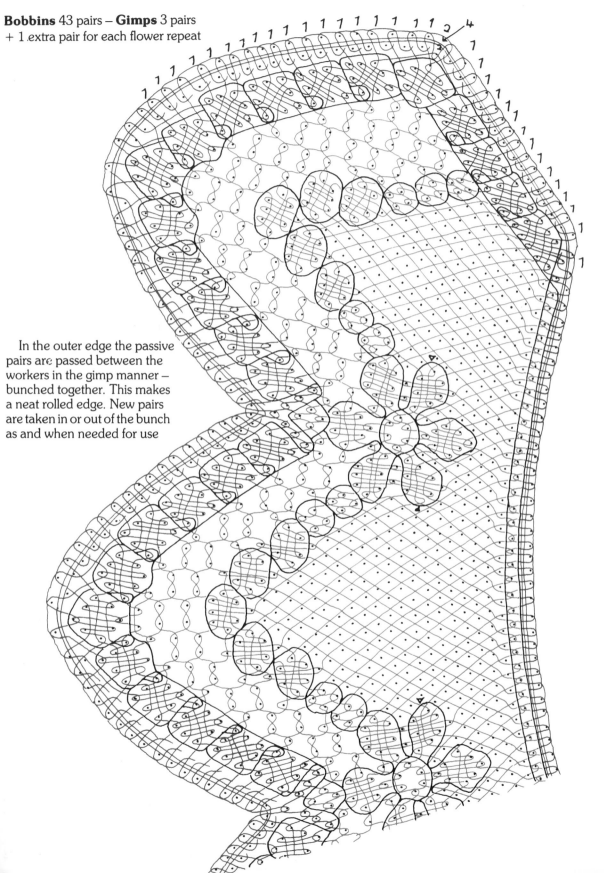

EMERALDS AND PEARLS

Bobbins 44 pairs – **Gimps** 3 pairs

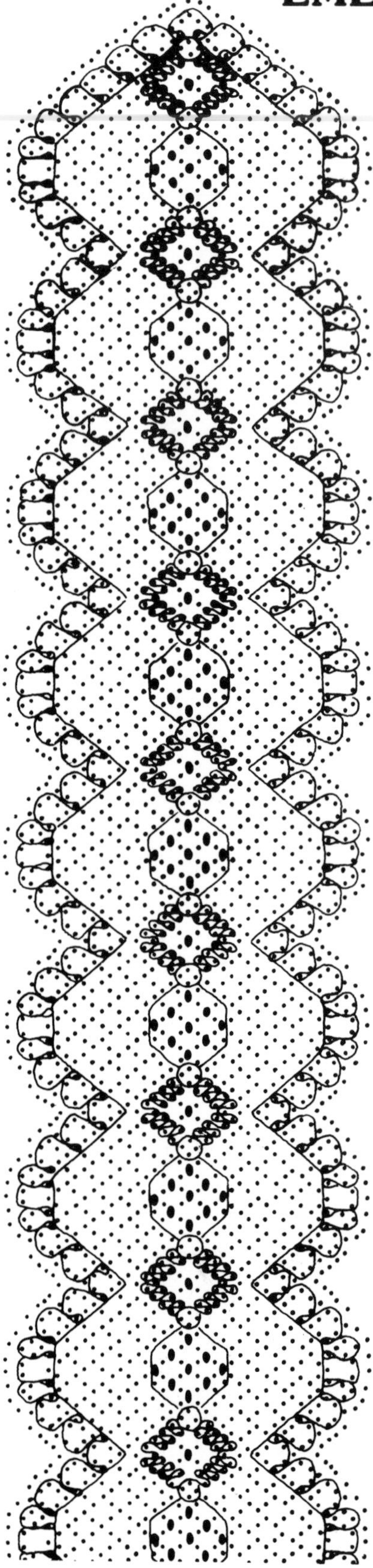

The net is an alternate
honeycomb – worked
outwards to both sides,
left and right

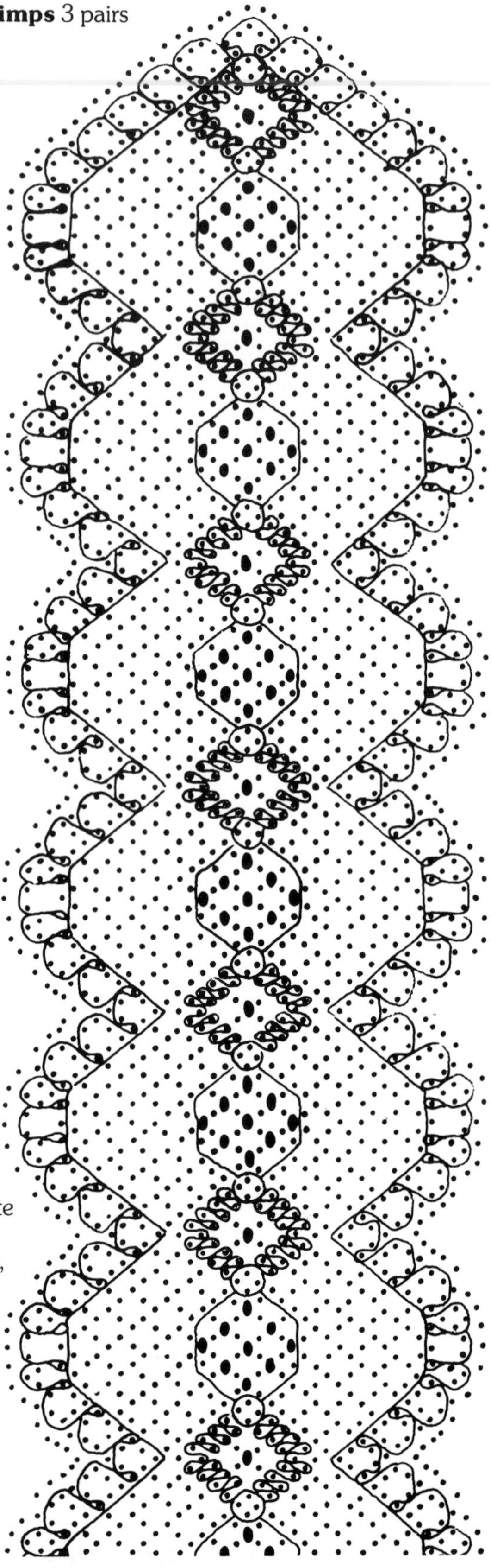

EMERALDS AND PEARLS

Bobbins 44 pairs – **Gimps** 3 pairs

After all the pairs have been added on the outer edges the pairs are bunched and passed between the workers as in gimp work. The hexagonal shape is worked in whole stitch – the whole stitch being supported only on the pin

ACE OF SPADES

Bobbins 50 pairs – **Gimps** 3 pairs

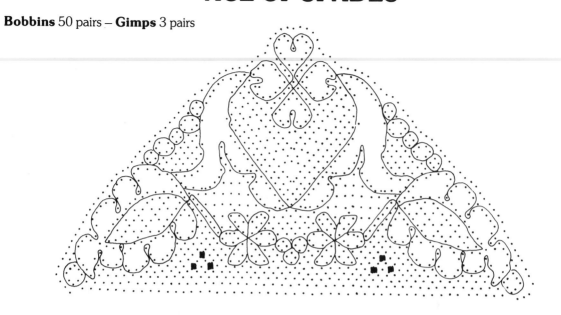

Handkerchief corner in three sizes

ACE OF SPADES

Bobbins 50 pairs – **Gimps** 3 pairs

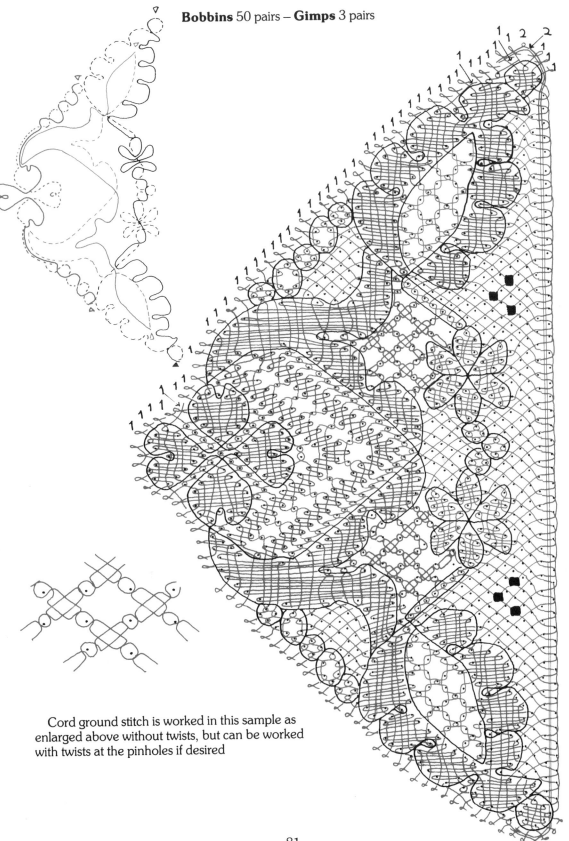

Cord ground stitch is worked in this sample as
enlarged above without twists, but can be worked
with twists at the pinholes if desired

SPRING FURROWS

Bobbins 42 pairs – **Gimps** 2 pairs

TRI-FLORA

Bobbins 50 pairs – **Gimps** 2 pairs for *edge*
4 pairs for *flower*

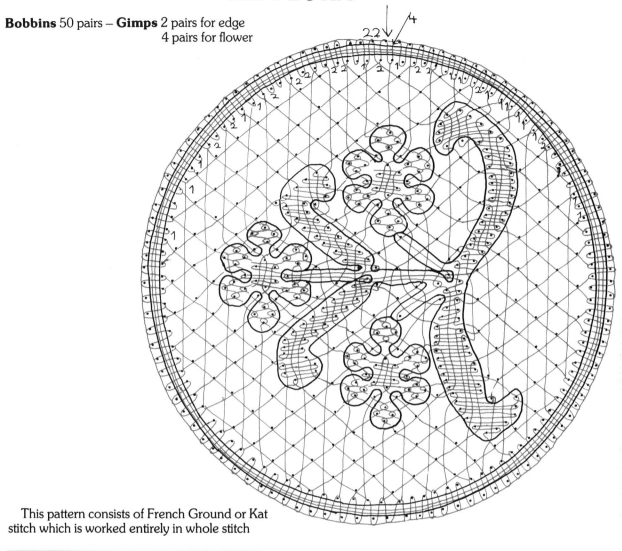

This pattern consists of French Ground or Kat
stitch which is worked entirely in whole stitch

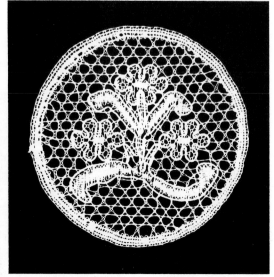

83

COMPASS

Bobbins 54 pairs – **Gimps** 2 pairs for edge
+ 3 pairs for motif

SUMMER ROSE

Bobbins 64 pairs – **Gimps** 6 pairs
+ 2 single

The rose has an unusual
honeycomb filling

85

HAPPY WEDDING

Bobbins 60 pairs – **Gimps** 2 pairs + 3 single
+ 3 extra for corner

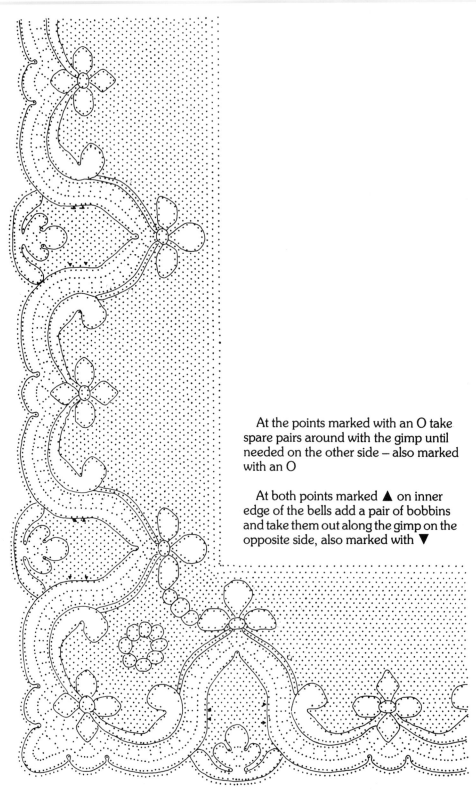

At the points marked with an O take
spare pairs around with the gimp until
needed on the other side – also marked
with an O

At both points marked ▲ on inner
edge of the bells add a pair of bobbins
and take them out along the gimp on the
opposite side, also marked with ▼

HAPPY WEDDING

Bobbins 60 pairs – **Gimps** 2 pairs + 3 single + 3 extra for corner

HAPPY WEDDING

Bobbins 60 pairs – **Gimps** 2 pairs + 3 single + 3 extra for corner

HAPPY WEDDING

Bobbins 60 pairs – **Gimps** 2 pairs + 3 single
+ 3 extra for corner

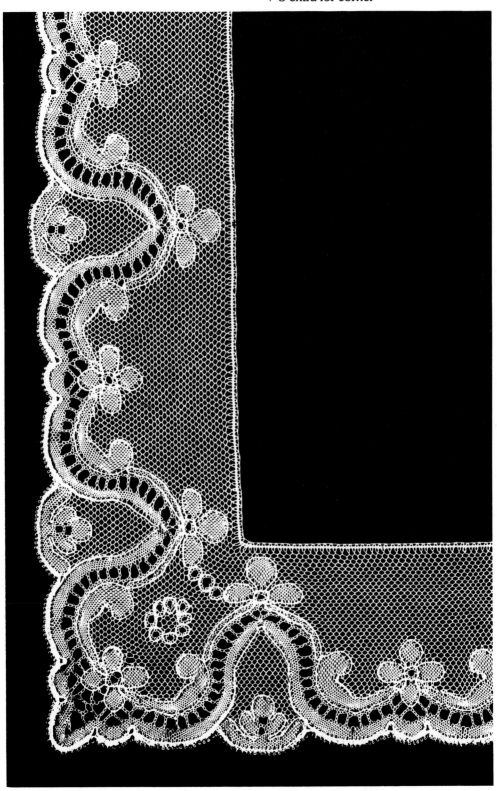

RAMBLING ROSE

Bobbins 60 pairs – **Gimps** 1 pair for edge + 6 pairs for each flower repeat
+ 3 extra pairs for the corner

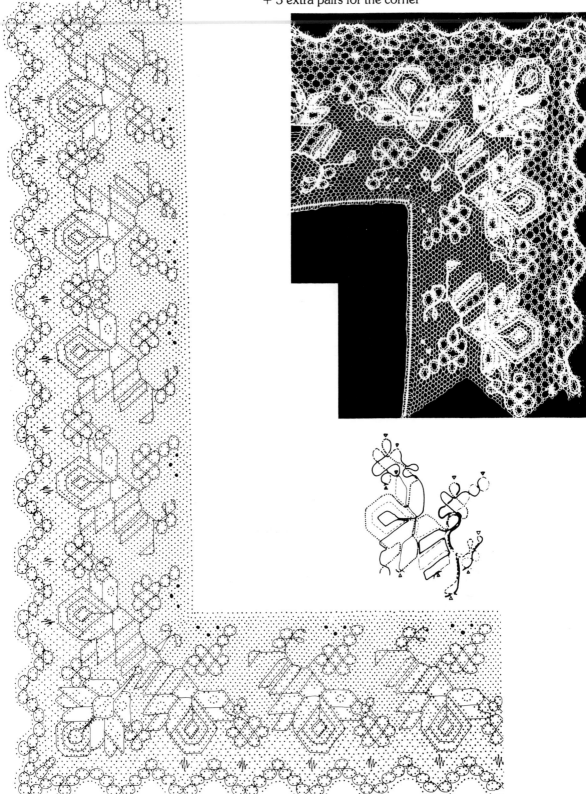

RAMBLING ROSE

Bobbins 60 pairs – **Gimps** 1 pair for edge + 6 pairs for each flower repeat
+ 3 extra pairs for the corner

Made in 180 cotton thread with DMC 16 as gimp thread

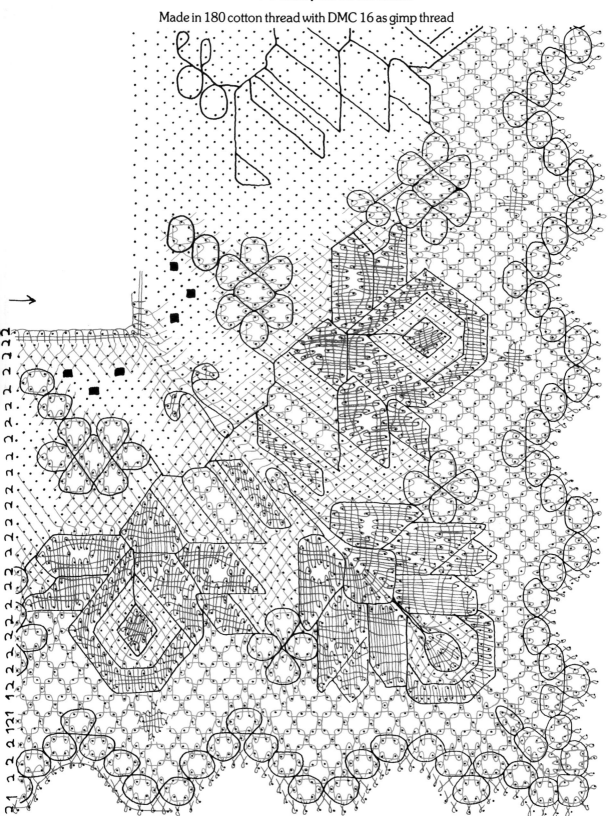

EVE

Bobbins 61 pairs – **Gimps** 2 pairs for edge
+ 5 pairs for flower

Three alternative sizes. The smallest size
needs to be worked in 180 thread

EVE

Bobbins 61 pairs – **Gimps** 2 pairs for edge
+ 5 pairs for flower

Care needs to be taken to ensure that the threads in the left-hand side flower pass through the gimp twice each time, so that the gimp is securely held

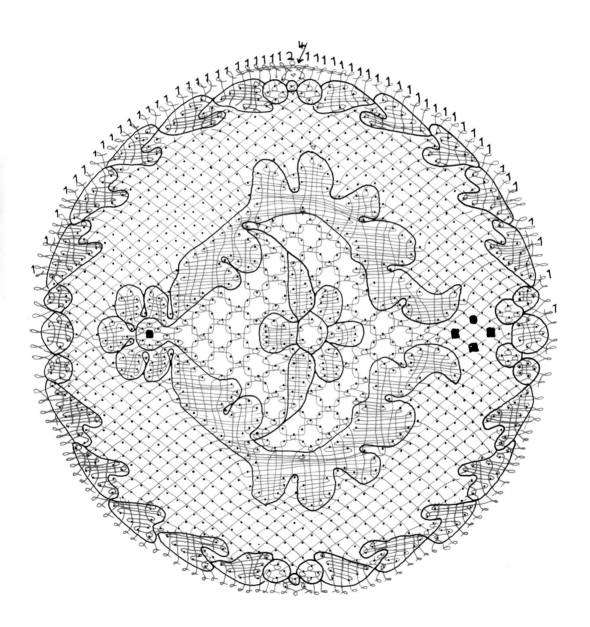

CANCER

Bobbins 68 pairs – **Gimps** 2 pairs for outer edge
+ 8 pairs for motif's centre

94

CANCER

Bobbins 68 pairs – **Gimps** 2 pairs for outer edge
+ 8 pairs for motif's centre

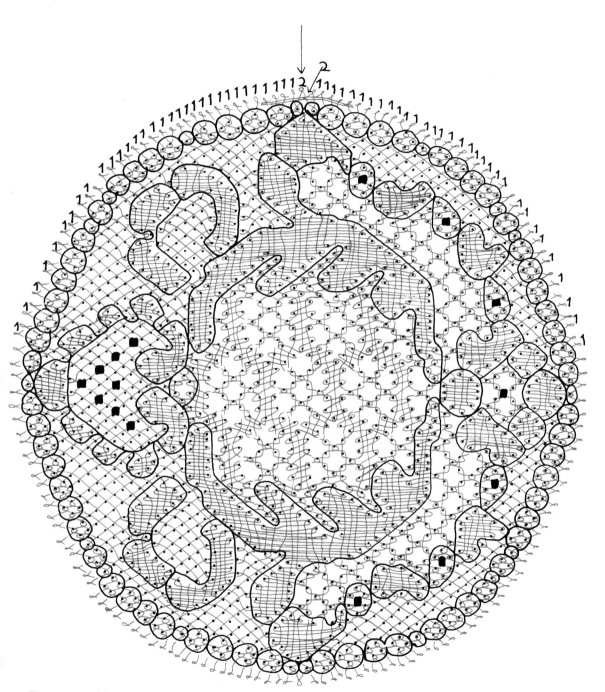

The centre of the motif has an unusual
filling of whole stitch trails leading into
honeycomb centres

95

CHRISTINE

Bobbins 69 pairs – **Gimps** 5 pairs for the outer edge and the trails
+ 11 pairs for each group of flower repeats

CHRISTINE

Bobbins 69 pairs – **Gimps** 5 pairs for the outer edge and the trails
+ 11 pairs for each group of flower repeats

The collar needs to be made in a fine thread – 120 or even finer. The pattern is reversed at the centre line; the small marked numbers on the diagram in the honeycomb rings indicate the number of bobbins needed to be started within that ring

Start at the inner corner and add pairs all along the top edge in the honeycomb rings; also add pairs where indicated in the first whole stitch trail

CHRISTINE

Bobbins 69 pairs – **Gimps** 5 pairs for the outer edge and the trails
+ 11 pairs for each group of flower repeats

CHRISTINE

Bobbins 69 pairs – **Gimps** 5 pairs for the outer edge and the trails
+ 11 pairs for each group of flower repeats

GRIDS

These grids can be used to
enable lacemakers to create the
own designs

This grid, drawn at 52°,
illustrates the 45° turn at a corne

No footside marked

20 pinholes to a 10 cm length

Footside
marked

20 pinholes to a
10 cm length

Footside marked

52°. 32 pinholes to a 10 cm length

Footside marked

52°. 32 pinholes to a 10 cm length

BOOK SUPPLIERS

ENGLAND
The following are stockists of the complete Batsford/Dryad Press range. For an expanded list, including equipment suppliers, please write to the Publishers.

Avon
Bridge Bookshop
7 Bridge Street
Bath BA2 4AS

Waterstone & Co.
4-5 Milsom Street
Bath BA1 1DA

Bedfordshire
Arthur Sells
Lane Cove
49 Pedley Lane
Clifton
Shefford SG17 5QT

Berkshire
Loricraft
4 Big Lane
Lambourn
Berkshire

West End Lace Supplies
Ravensworth Court Road
Mortimer West End
Reading RG7 3UD

Buckinghamshire
J.S. Sear Lacecraft Supplies
8 Hillview
Sheringham MK16 9NY

Cambridgeshire
Dillons the Bookstore
Sidney Street
Cambridge

Cheshire
Lyn Turner
Church Meadow Crafts
15 Carisbrook Drive
Winsford CW7 1LN

Devon
Creative Crafts & Needlework
18 High Street
Totnes TQ9 5NP

Honiton Lace Shop
44 High Street
Honiton EX14 8PJ

Dorset
F. Herring & Sons
High West Street
Dorchester DT1 1UP

Tim Parker (mail order)
124 Corhampton Road
Boscombe East
Bournemouth BH6 5NL

Christopher Williams
19 Morrison Avenue
Parkstone
Poole BH17 4AD

Durham
Lacemaid
6, 10, & 15 Stoneybeck
Bishop Middleham DL17 9BL

Gloucestershire
Southgate Handicrafts
63 Southgate Street
Gloucester GL1 1TX

Waterstone & Co.
89-90 The Promenade
Cheltenham GL50 1NB

Hampshire
Creative Crafts
11 The Square
Winchester SO23 9ES

Doreen Gill
14 Barnfield Road
Petersfield GU31 4DR

Larkfield Crafts
4 Island Cottages
Mapledurwell
Basingstoke RG23 2LU

Needlestyle
24-26 West Street
Alresford

Ruskins
27 Bell Street
Romsey

Isle of Wight
Busy Bobbins
Unit 7
Scarrots Lane
Newport PO30 1JD

Kent
The Handicraft Shop
47 Northgate
Canterbury

Frances Iles
73 High Street
Rochester ME1 1LX

Lincolnshire
Rippingale Lace
Barn Farm House
off Station Road
Rippingdale Bourne

London
Foyles
119 Charing Cross Road
WC2H 0EB

Hatchards
187 Piccadilly W1

Middlesex
Redburn Crafts
Squires Garden Centre
Halliford Road
Upper Halliford
Shepperton TW17 8RU

Norfolk
Alby Lace Museum
Cromer Road
Alby
Norwich NR11 7QE

Jane's Pincushions
Taverham Craft Unit 4
Taverham Nursery Centre
Fir Covert Road
Taverham
Norwich NR8 6HT

Waterstone & Co.
30 London Street
Norwich NR2 1LD

Northamptonshire
D.J. Hornsby
149 High Street
Burton Latimer
Kettering NN15 5RL

Staffordshire
J. & J. Ford
October Hill
65 Upper Way
Upper Longdon
Rugeley WS16 1QB

Surrey
Needlestyle
5 The Woolmead
Farnham GU9 1TN

Sussex
Southern Handicrafts
20 Kensington Gardens
Brighton BN1 4AL

Warwickshire
Christine & David Springett
21 Hillmorton Road
Rugby CV22 6DF

North Yorkshire
Shireburn Lace
Finkel Court
Finkel Hill
Sherburn in Elmet LS25 6EB

Valley House Craft Studios
Ruston
Scarborough

West Midlands
Needlewoman
Needles Alley
off New Street
Birmingham

West Yorkshire
Sebalace
Waterloo Mill
Howden Road
Silsden BD20 0HA

George White Lacemaking
   Supplies
40 Heath Drive
Boston Spa LS23 6PB

Jo Firth
58 Kent Crescent
Lowtown, Pudsey
Leeds LS28 9EB

Wales
Bryncraft Bobbins
B.J. Phillips
Pantglas
Cellan
Lampeter
Dyfed SA48 BJD

Scotland
Embroidery Shop
51 Withain Street
Edinburgh
Lothian EH3 7LW

Beverley Scarlett
Strupak
Hillhead
Coldwells
Ellon
Aberdeenshire

Waterstone & Co.
236 Union Street
Aberdeen AB1 1TN

INDEX